WELS and Other Lutherans:

Lutheran Church Bodies in the USA

John F. Brug

Edward C. Fredrich II

Armin W. Schuetze

NORTHWESTERN PUBLISHING HOUSE
Milwaukee, Wisconsin

Fourth printing, 1998
Third printing, 1995
Second printing, 1995

Library of Congress Card 94-74993
Northwestern Publishing House
1250 N. 113th St., Milwaukee, WI 53226-3284

Published 1995
Printed in the United States of America
ISBN 0-8100-0543-3

Table of Contents

• ✣ ✣ ✣ •

Introduction

Lutheranism moved from Europe to America by means of a long series of migrations, which spanned three centuries. The immigrants founded dozens of Lutheran church bodies, which preached the gospel in nearly a dozen languages. Through the years these groups experienced a bewildering array of mergers, splits, and reconciliations.

In 1995 the net result of all this action and interaction is two large Lutheran church bodies which number in the millions, namely, The Lutheran Church—Missouri Synod and The Evangelical Lutheran Church in America; one medium-sized church body which numbers in the hundreds of thousands, that is, The Wisconsin Evangelical Lutheran Synod; and about twenty small church bodies which individually count their membership only in the tens of thousands, the thousands, or even the hundreds.

The aim of this book is to provide a brief, popular overview of these church bodies. Where did they come from? What is their doctrinal position today? What are the differences which cause them to remain separate?

The intended readership is lay people who are seeking basic, introductory information about these church bodies. No extensive documentation or footnotes are provided in the main text, but each major section will conclude with a few suggestions for further study for the benefit of readers who wish to make a more thorough investigation of the subject.

INTRODUCTION

This study is not written from the viewpoint of a detached, neutral historian, but from the doctrinal perspective of the Wisconsin Synod. It is written primarily to inform members of that church body about the relationship of their church to the other Lutherans of America.

This study has three major sections, each of which was produced primarily by one of the three authors. These sections necessarily differ in style and scope because of the difference of subject matter.

In Part One, Armin Schuetze reviews the century-long relationship of the Lutheran Church—Missouri Synod and the Wisconsin Evangelical Lutheran Synod from the time of their first contacts until the breakup of the Synodical Conference in 1963. He also briefly presents the doctrinal differences which continue to keep them apart thirty years after that breakup.

Part Two traces the complicated series of mergers which by 1988 had swept nearly all of the Lutheran church bodies in the United States into one large church, The Evangelical Lutheran Church in America. It also demonstrates the great doctrinal gap which separates the ELCA from the Wisconsin Synod and the Missouri Synod. John Brug is the author of this section.

The Missouri Synod and the ELCA contain approximately 94 percent of the Lutherans in the United States. The WELS is the home of about 5 percent. In recent years the percentage of American Lutherans in the WELS and other smaller bodies has been increasing. This is not due to a great increase in the size of these smaller groups, but to a serious membership decline in the major bodies.

In Part Three, Edward C. Fredrich II provides capsule descriptions of sixteen of the small Lutheran bodies which comprise about 1 percent of American Lutheranism. These brief descriptions focus on the "reason for being" which keeps these bodies independent of the larger Lutheran churches.

Within the WELS, questions about other Lutheran churches in America usually arise when our members come into contact with these other Lutheran church bodies through friends or relatives. It is the authors' hope that this little volume will serve as a ready reference in such circumstances.

PART ONE

WELS

AND

The Lutheran Church— Missouri Synod

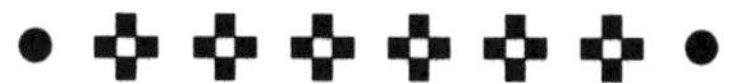

PART ONE

WELS and the Missouri Synod

The Wisconsin Evangelical Lutheran Synod (WELS) was founded in 1850 by congregations in and around Milwaukee, Wisconsin. When it merged with the Minnesota and Michigan Synods, its membership spread over the midwestern states. Although the synod has expanded its work since the mid-1900s so that its 420,000 baptized members are now found in congregations throughout the United States and in several provinces of Canada, it continues to have a very high percentage of its membership concentrated in Wisconsin, Minnesota, and Michigan.

Since 1863 the synod has conducted a seminary for the training of its pastors. At present two preparatory schools and one college round out the synod's educational system for the thorough training of its pastors and teachers. Since World War II the WELS has expanded its world mission effort into more than fifteen countries.

The Lutheran Church—Missouri Synod (LCMS) was organized in Chicago in 1847. The name "Missouri Synod" was derived from the "home base" of the synod's founders, a group of Saxon immigrants who had settled in St. Louis and in Perry County, Missouri, after fleeing from Germany in order to escape government pressure to compromise their Lutheran convictions. The second key component in the founding of the LCMS was a group of missionaries sent to America from Germany by W. Loehe. Their work centered in Michigan and adjacent states.

The founder and first leader of the Missouri Synod was C. F. W. Walther, who had emerged as the leader of the Saxon immigrants. Walther quickly established himself as the leading spokesman for strong, confessional Lutheranism in America. His clear, firm doctrinal position strengthened confessional Lutheranism in America and, indeed, throughout the world.

The synod experienced rapid growth as it quickly expanded into many states, even beyond the middle west. By 1884 it had nearly 350,000 baptized members. By 1935 it had grown to over one and a quarter million. Its present membership is 2,600,000. This membership is well dispersed throughout the United States. The state of Missouri ranks well down the list with only half as many LCMS members as Illinois, the leading state. Among the midwestern states Michigan, Minnesota, and Wisconsin all rank ahead of Missouri in LCMS membership. In fact, the LCMS has significantly more members in these three states than the WELS.

Unlike ELCA, the LCMS is primarily the result of internal growth, rather than merger. The LCMS has an extensive system of Christian education, culminating in ten colleges or universities and two seminaries. The LCMS has missions or sister churches in more than 30 countries.

For nearly a century, from 1868 to 1961, the WELS and the LCMS were in church or confessional fellowship. Besides practicing pulpit and altar fellowship, they carried on joint educational and mission projects. This ended in 1961. What originally brought these two synods together? On what basis did they practice fellowship? What caused the break in fellowship? What is the present situation?

A. Past Relations

In establishing fellowship in 1868 as well as in declaring the fellowship bonds broken in 1961, the doctrine of church fellowship and a practice consistent with Scripture were decisive factors. From its very beginning the LCMS was firmly committed to orthodox, confessional Lutheranism. Its confessional basis was "Holy Scripture of the Old Testament and New Testament as the written Word of God and only rule and norm of faith and life, and all the Lutheran Confessions as the pure and unadulterated explanation and presentation of the divine word." Dr. C. F. W. Walther, already known for his faithfulness to Scripture and the Confessions, was chosen as the first president. Under his capable leadership, especially also as seminary president, the Missouri Synod grew into the outstanding confessional Lutheran church body in America. This showed itself also in the synod's fellowship practice. It was not until 1868 that the Missouri Synod was ready to recognize the Wisconsin Synod, founded in 1850, as a sister synod with whom it could practice church fellowship.

At its founding the Wisconsin Synod, under its first president, Pastor John Muehlhaeuser, represented a mild Lutheranism, committed to Scripture and the gospel but with less emphasis on the Lutheran Confessions. Through its first founders it was associated with the German mission societies. Among these mission societies the confessional differences between Lutheran and Reformed were not a hindrance to joint communion. However, very soon, when Pastor John Bading became president (1860) and with the advent of Dr. Adolph Hoenecke as theological leader, the synod broke its ties with the mission societies and embraced a sound confessional Lutheranism. Only then did the Missouri Synod enter into fellowship with the Wisconsin Synod. Thus, it was especially in their doctrine and practice of fellowship that these two synods showed each other that they were serious about their commitment to Scripture and the Confessions. Until they were agreed on this, the Missouri Synod did not consider the Wisconsin Synod an orthodox Lutheran synod with whom it could make common cause.

Once agreement had been reached, both synods very soon played prominent roles in founding the Synodical Conference of North America (1872). This conference was committed to the same doctrinal, confessional position held by Missouri and Wisconsin and the other synods uniting in this federation. These synods were disappointed in the General Council (organized in 1867). While the council sought to bring together into one body the synods who wanted to be soundly confessional, it failed to commit itself to scriptural practice in regard to pulpit and altar fellowship as well as lodge membership and complete agreement in doctrine. The doctrine and practice of fellowship were at stake.

Although in its early decades a controversy over the doctrines of predestination and conversion resulted in several defections from the Synodical Conference, the WELS and the LCMS remained united in contending for the full truth of Scripture. It was not until the 1930s and '40s that problems arose.

In 1938 after a series of discussions the Missouri Synod was ready to accept two documents as a basis for fellowship with the recently formed American Lutheran Church (1930), although these two documents did not, in fact, settle the former doctrinal differences. By 1944 the LCMS approved a resolution that allowed for a distinction between prayer fellowship and joint prayers that were not an expression of fellowship. If, for example, professors, students, or editors of the LCMS would meet with professors, students, or editors from Lutheran bodies with whom they were not in doctrinal agreement, joint devotions and prayers in connection with such meetings were not considered fellowship. The WELS considered them unionistic. Soon the application of Romans 16:17,18 "to all Christians who differ from us in certain points of doctrine" was challenged by prominent pastors and professors of the Missouri Synod. Although full doctrinal agreement had not been achieved with the ALC, joint activities that were not merely cooperation in externals increased and soon involved the practice of joint worship. This was true especially on the part of chaplains serving in the armed services. As to cooperation in externals, the WELS too recognized that one could cooperate with other Lutherans in the external activity of sending relief supplies to the poor in war-torn Europe. This, however, never involved joint worship and prayer.

When, after a period of more than 20 years, differences between the WELS and the LCMS in the doctrine and practice of church fellowship could not be resolved, the WELS in 1961 acknowledged and declared the break in fellowship.

Other differences, somewhat related, arose during those years. Missouri chose to cooperate with other Lutherans and the government in the military chaplaincy. Wisconsin chose to go the route of having its own civilian chaplains to avoid fellowship problems and confusion of church and state.

Missouri changed its practice in regard to the Boy Scout movement. It resolved that congregations might have their own troops, enabling them to control anything that might be objectionable. Wisconsin found the mandatory Scout Oath and Scout Law objectionable because of their inherent self-righteous spirit. But these had to be used also in church-related troops. Wisconsin chose to develop its own program in the Lutheran Pioneers.

By 1961 professors at Missouri's Concordia Seminary, St. Louis, were promoting the use of the historical-critical method of Bible interpretation. According to this method, Scripture is to be interpreted critically like any other literature. Thus, for example, the creation account is not to be understood as history that really happened; science has proved otherwise. The miracles of Jesus are stories of the early Christians rather than true accounts of what Jesus did. The use of this method of interpretation raised questions about Missouri's doctrine of the Bible's inspiration and complete inerrancy.

During the decades before 1961 the doctrines of the church and the ministry were discussed. Both synods agreed on the doctrine of the invisible church, consisting of all believers. As to visible groups, Missouri considered the local congregation the one divinely instituted visible form of the church. Wisconsin, however, saw no such limitation in Scripture and considered a synod to be church in the same sense as a local congregation is church. Whether Christians unite in a synod or in a local congregation to do the Lord's work, in either case it is in accord with the will of God.

Both synods also were agreed on the priesthood of all believers, that God has committed his gospel to all believers. As to the public ministry, Missouri considered the pastorate in the local congregation the only divinely instituted office. Wisconsin, while recognizing that God instituted the public ministry of the gospel, found no direct word of institution in Scripture for any particular form of this ministry, such as the pastorate in a local congregation. Teachers, professors, synod and district presidents, administrators, etc. also receive a divine call into the public ministry no less than pastors. These are all God-pleasing forms of the divinely instituted public ministry.

When the break in fellowship came in 1961, discussions on these doctrines had not reached a conclusion. As the two synods attempted to resolve their differences, the subject of church fellowship was more urgent and preempted their time and energy and became the primary cause for the break.

B. The Present Situation

1. Fellowship

The doctrine of church fellowship continues as a major divisive issue between the WELS and the LCMS.

The WELS continues to believe and teach that confessional agreement in all that Scripture teaches is required for the practice of religious fellowship in all its forms. The WELS recognizes that the same scriptural principles (based on Matthew 7:15-19; 2 Timothy 2:17-19; 2 John 9-11; Romans 16:17,18) apply, whether this is "by joint worship, by joint proclamation of the Gospel, by joining in Holy Communion, by joint prayer, by joint church work." In that sense, church or religious fellowship has been referred to as a "unit concept" in that its practice in all its forms is under the same biblical directives.

The LCMS officially teaches that full agreement in doctrine is required for pulpit and altar fellowship. This is seen as referring primarily to participating in the regular and official public and corporate worship services of a congregation. But the LCMS does not apply this principle to occasional joint gatherings at which worship does take place as, for example, "joint Christian celebrations, gatherings, rallies, convocations, commencements, baccalaureates, dedications, exhibitions, pageants, concerts, colloquia, conferences, and other public events."

Thus the LCMS promotes and practices "levels" or "degrees" of fellowship. This means that some expressions of fellowship (for example, pulpit and altar fellowship) require a greater degree of agreement than others (for example, prayer).

A former president of the LCMS expressed this as follows: "Complete agreement on confessional doctrine and practice is neither possible nor necessary for every inter-Christian or inter-denominational action. Expressions of Christian unity should be proportionate to the measure of consensus in confessing the Biblical Gospel we enjoy with the other Christians involved. Although this point has seldom been articulated in official synodical documents, it has in fact been practiced by the Missouri Synod for many years." In 1991 the LCMS Commission on Theology and Church Relations gave similar expression to this view: "On the basis of the Biblical principles of fellowship we must insist that expressions of Christian unity be proportionate to the measure of consensus in confessing the Biblical Gospel that we enjoy with the other Christians involved. While not articulated in detail in official synodical documents, this has been in fact the Synod's way of proceeding for many years."

In both of the above quotations there is the admission that the principle of "degrees of fellowship" ("expressions of Christian unity be proportionate to the measure of consensus in confessing the Biblical Gospel") was practiced in the LCMS for many years before it was "articulated in synodical documents." What in effect has happened is that unscriptural practice continued without being corrected. But this practice is now articulated in synodical documents with the claim that it is based "on Biblical principles of fellowship," although in its earlier history the LCMS rejected those same practices as unbiblical. Thus unbiblical practices that were not corrected have led to an unbiblical doctrine of church fellowship.

The following are some examples of unscriptural fellowship practices:

- Congregations of the LCMS set up joint worship services with congregations with whom they are not in formal pulpit and altar fellowship as, for example, joint Reformation services and other rallies or convocations.

- At what have been called "ecumenical wedding services" pastors or priests of churches not in fellowship with the LCMS congregation have been permitted to participate in the wedding service, perhaps by reading a portion of Scripture, by speaking a prayer or blessing.
- Although the official position of the LCMS holds to close(d) communion as scriptural, many of its congregations practice "open" communion to a greater or lesser degree by receiving at their altars Christians from church bodies with whom they are not in doctrinal agreement. Repeated efforts on the part of synod resolutions and published writings calling for close(d) communion do not appear to have corrected this unscriptural practice.

Thus, the LCMS doctrine of fellowship and its present practice no longer agree with the principles once confessed and practiced as revealed in Holy Scripture. This leads to a laxness in doctrinal discipline. The result is a pluralistic church in which a variety of doctrinal positions may be tolerated within the fellowship, even though the official position of the church may give the impression of orthodoxy.

2. Scouting

The WELS continues to oppose membership in the Boy Scouts of America because the mandatory Scout Oath and Scout Law promote a spirit of self-righteousness. This is contrary to the gospel of free salvation through the grace of God as shown in Christ's atoning sacrifice for sin.

The LCMS not only has Scout troops in its congregations where it believes it can eliminate what may be objectionable but allows membership in troops not under the church's jurisdiction.

3. Military Chaplaincy

Neither synod has changed its position regarding the military chaplaincy. The WELS continues to call civilian pastors to serve our men and women in the military. The LCMS continues to supply pastors who are commissioned by the government and serve under the government's regulations. This results in practices that are not in keeping with scriptural principles of church fellowship.

4. Scripture

As noted earlier, for a time it appeared that the LCMS was departing from the doctrine of the full and complete inspiration and inerrancy of Holy Scripture. An increasing number of professors, especially at the St. Louis seminary, promoted the historical-critical method of Bible interpretation which is not in keeping with the inerrant view of Scripture.

In 1974 the St. Louis seminary president, who was a leader among the professors with liberal views of Scripture, was suspended from his position. As a result, in what is called the "exodus," 90 percent of the faculty and 85 percent of the students left the St. Louis campus to form what was called Seminex (seminary-in-exile). Only five professors and a small percentage of students remained to begin rebuilding the St. Louis Concordia Seminary, purged of its liberal faction.

This appears to have rid the LCMS of those who questioned the full inspiration and inerrancy of the Bible. The "exodus" was a major event that turned the seminary in the right direction. The crisis at St. Louis showed that the LCMS wants to continue holding a sound view of Scripture and its proper interpretation. The question, however, is whether pastors who were trained by and share the views of the professors who walked out continue to serve in LCMS congregations.

There is little evidence that doctrinal discipline has been consistently carried out.

5. Church and Ministry

The WELS continues to teach that Scripture sets up no particular form of the church or of the public ministry as specifically instituted by God. God has not given his New Testament church such ecclesiastical, ceremonial directives.

The present LCMS position on the doctrine of the church and the ministry is unclear and uncertain. There are some who hold a position like that of the WELS. Others hold a modified LCMS view, recognizing, for example, that certain professors may have a divine call. The official position does seem to hold, however, to what was described above that there is a special divine institution for the local congregation and the pastorate in the congregation. This has at times caused some problems in practicing doctrinal discipline on the synodical level. Since according to this view only the congregation is a divinely instituted form of the church, the synod and its officials can practice discipline only according to the regulations established by the synod. Consequently, church discipline according to Scripture can be carried out only on the congregational level.

Thus, lack of agreement between the WELS and the LCMS on the doctrine of the church and the ministry continues. As was noted, this can have important practical implications.

6. The Role of Women in the Church

A more recent issue pertains to the role of women in the church. There is no question about the equal redemption Christ gained for all people, that "there is neither . . . male nor female, for you are all one in Christ Jesus" (Galatians 3:28). In God's kingdom men and women are fully equal, equal children of God through faith in the one Redeemer of all, equal heirs of salvation.

For many years LCMS and WELS were also agreed in teaching that the Lord, however, at the time of creation had assigned specific roles to man and woman, a leadership or headship role to man and a helping and submitting role to woman. There was agreement that passages like 1 Corinthians 14:34: "Women should remain silent in the church. They are not allowed to speak, but must be in submission, as the Law says," and 1 Timothy 2:11,12: "Woman should learn in quietness and full submission. I do not permit a woman to teach or to have authority over a man; she must be silent," required that only men should serve as pastors and in leadership roles, and that consequently voting rights in the congregations should be restricted to the male members.

In 1969 the LCMS changed its position in regard to woman suffrage. Since then, women have not only been given the right to vote but have been placed into positions of authority including that of serving on the synod's board of directors. Only the office of the pastor, who is entrusted with the means of grace, is looked upon as prohibited to women in the above passages. Surveys, however, have indicated that a growing number of pastors and lay people also favor calling women as pastors.

Thus, the role of women in the church has become an issue between the two synods since 1961 when the separation occurred.

Summary

There are important doctrines and practices that stand between the WELS and the LCMS: church fellowship with its many applications, the Boy Scout issue, the military chaplaincy, the doctrines of church and ministry, the role of women in the church.

Because of these differences no church or religious fellowship is practiced between the two synods. The WELS must apply what Scripture says about fellowship. Pastors of the two synods do not preach in each other's pulpits; members do not attend the Lord's Supper in each other's churches; no joint worship, no joint prayer, no joint religious work is carried on.

All of this is not to deny the presence of sincere pastors and teachers and many sincere believers in the LCMS. We will pray for them. We will use whatever opportunities the Lord provides to witness the truth in love, to remove the differences that divide us. We eagerly look forward to experiencing with them the blessed and perfect fellowship we will enjoy in heaven.

A Summary of Differences in the Teachings of WELS and LCMS

WELS	LCMS
1. Agreement on all scriptural teachings is required for all forms of fellowship.	1. Full agreement in doctrine is required only for pulpit and altar fellowship.
2. Same scriptural principles apply to all forms of church or religious fellowship.	2. Full agreement is not necessary for worship at occasional joint Christian celebrations, Reformation services, convocations, rallies, etc.
3. All joint prayer is an expression of fellowship.	3. There can be joint prayer that is not an act of fellowship.
4. Only pastors in doctrinal agreement can officiate at weddings.	4. Some pastors allow "ecumenical wedding services" at which pastors

WELS	LCMS
	or priests not in fellowship with LCMS may participate.
5. Only those in confessional agreement may receive the Lord's Supper together (close[d] communion).	5. Official position holds to close(d) communion, but numerous pastors and churches practice "open communion" allowing joint communion with those not in doctrinal agreement.
6. Opposes membership in Boy Scouts of America because of mandatory Scout Oath and Scout Law which promote a spirit of self-righteousness.	6. Allows membership in scout troops.
7. Conducts own Pioneer program for children in congregations.	7. Congregations conduct Boy Scout troops hoping to eliminate objectionable features.
8. Sees government military chaplaincy as a violation of separation of church and state, as incompatible with the divine call, and opening the door to unionistic practices.	8. Sees no doctrinal problems in the government chaplaincy.
9. Calls and funds civilian chaplains when needed and possible.	9. Calls pastors to serve as government funded and commissioned chaplains.

WELS	LCMS
10. No particular form of the visible church is divinely instituted. The invisible church is present in the local congregation and the synod. Both can be called church in the same sense.	10. Official position seems to be that the local congregation is the one divinely instituted form of the visible church. By contrast the synod is a human arrangement.
11. Both the congregation and the synod may exercise church discipline on the basis of Scripture.	11. The synod and its officials can practice discipline only according to the regulations adopted by the synod.
12. The pastor of a local congregation is only one form of the divinely instituted public ministry. Other forms are teachers, professors, called administrators, etc. The specific form is determined by the church's call.	12. Official position seems to be that the only divinely instituted form of the public ministry is that of pastor in a local congregation. All other positions are auxiliary to this.
13. Because Scripture assigns a headship role to man and a helping role to woman, women do not participate in voting at congregational meetings.	13. Women are granted full voting rights.
14. Only men may serve as pastors and in other leadership roles that	14. Women may not serve as pastors but may serve on the church

WELS	LCMS
exercise authority over men.	council, the synod board of directors, and other leadership positions.
15. Scripture is the inspired, inerrant Word of God. There are no errors in the Bible.	15. Seems to have overcome problem at seminary, eliminating the historical critical method of Bible interpretation which allows for errors in the Bible and attempts to harmonize Scripture and science (reason) (e.g., allowing for evolution). Question remains whether it has also been overcome among pastors throughout the synod.

For Further Reading

Fredrich, Edward C. II, *The Wisconsin Synod Lutherans,* Milwaukee: Northwestern Publishing House, 1992, especially pp. 175-185, 198-207.

Fredrich, Edward C. II, "Trumpet with a Certain Sound: The Synodical Conference's Confessional Commitment," *Wisconsin Lutheran Quarterly,* Vol. 90, Winter 1993, pp. 14-32.

Gawrisch, Wilbert R., "'Levels of Fellowship'—Scriptural Principles or Rules of Men?" *Wisconsin Lutheran Quarterly,* Vol. 88, Winter 1991, pp. 3-14.

Nass, Thomas P. and Lyle W. Lange, "'Inter-Christian Relationships'—An Evaluation," *Wisconsin Lutheran Quarterly,* Vol. 89, Summer 1992, pp. 217-220.

Schuetze, Armin W., "The WELS and the LCMS—Where Are We Now?" *Wisconsin Lutheran Quarterly,* Vol. 85, Fall 1988, pp. 261-286.

PART TWO

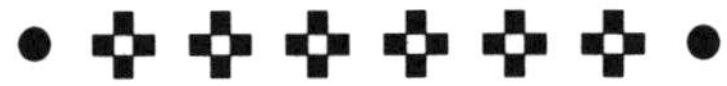

WELS

AND

The Evangelical Lutheran Church in America

PART TWO

WELS and the Evangelical Lutheran Church in America

With more than 5 million members The Evangelical Lutheran Church in America (ELCA) is the largest Lutheran church in the United States. It is the second largest Lutheran church in the world, trailing only the state church of Sweden. It has more than 11,000 congregations, which were organized into 65 synods. Its greatest concentration of members is located in an arc anchored by Pennsylvania and Ohio at one end and Minnesota, Iowa, and the Dakotas at the other end.

The ELCA is one of the newest Lutheran churches since it is the product of a 1988 merger of the Lutheran Church in America (LCA), the American Lutheran Church (ALC), and the Association of Evangelical Lutheran Churches (AELC). However, the ELCA includes in its membership the oldest Lutheran churches in America, churches whose history extends back before the American Revolution.

The Evangelical Lutheran Church in America (ELCA) is a merger of mergers. ELCA has swallowed up nearly all of the previous mergers of American Lutheranism (See Appendix 1). The Lutheran Church—Missouri Synod is the only large Lutheran church in the United States which remains outside this merger. The Wisconsin Synod makes up the greatest part of the remaining Lutherans who have shunned the big mergers or who have fled from various mergers along the road to Lutheran union.

The ELCA is the American Lutheran church which has departed the farthest from the doctrinal position of confessional Lutheranism. Some of the church bodies which merged into ELCA were the pioneers in introducing negative criticism of the Bible and compromising ecumenical tendencies into American Lutheranism. However, some of the Lutheran churches swallowed up in ELCA were once quite close to the doctrinal position of the old Synodical Conference. At one time the doctrinal differences between the Wisconsin Synod and some of the predecessor bodies of ELCA involved disagreement about non-fundamental doctrines of Scripture, such as church fellowship, millennialism, and the antichrist. Today the wide gap which separates the Wisconsin Synod from ELCA involves the most fundamental doctrines of Scripture.

To see how this doctrinal gap widened we will undertake a two-step study of ELCA. Before we examine the present doctrinal state of ELCA, we will look at the doctrinal heritage which ELCA has received from the synods and churches which preceded it so that we can compare and contrast ELCA's present position with its past.

A. The Predecessors of the ELCA

The history of American Lutheranism confronts us with a confusing tangle of mergers, splits, and remergers. But we need to understand at least the basic trends of this process if we are to understand how American Lutheranism got to its present state. As we survey this history, we will see in ELCA the sad, but inevitable, culmination of trends which have been present in American Lutheranism from the beginning, but we will also see a shocking degeneration from the doctrinal position which many of the predecessors of ELCA once held and defended.

We begin our study by tracing the origins of the church bodies that merged into the ELCA.

1. The LCA

The Lutheran Church in America (LCA) was the largest contributor to ELCA. Its 3 million members and 6,000 congregations were most heavily concentrated in Pennsylvania, Minnesota, and Illinois.

The LCA was more liberal in doctrine and had a longer heritage of liberalism than the other merging bodies. Its predecessor, the United Lutheran Church in America (ULCA), pioneered the acceptance of negative criticism of the Bible and the undermining of the doctrine of Scripture in American Lutheranism. The LCA merely carried on what the ULCA had begun. The ULCA/LCA's ecumenical efforts were the earliest and most far-ranging in American Lutheranism. They led the way in looking beyond inter-Protestant ecumenical efforts toward ties with Roman Catholicism and other churches with bishops. The LCA put a greater emphasis on the roles of pastors and the synod in the governing of the church. The LCA was the greatest contributor to the feminist, gay-rights, liberation theology lobbies which often hold ELCA hostage.

The ULCA contributed almost 80 percent of the membership of the LCA. The LCA, like the ULCA, was a true heir of the compromising party of old, eastern Lutheranism. The Swedish Augustana Evangelical Lutheran Church and the smaller Danish, Finnish, Slovak, and Icelandic churches which joined ULCA/LCA at various stages of the merger process were swallowed up in the theological liberalism of the united church.

a. The ULCA

The United Lutheran Church in America was the result of the 1918 merger of the three pieces of old, eastern Lutheranism: the General Synod, the General Council, and the United Synod, South. In many respects the formation of ELCA was simply the completion of the 1918 merger. From its beginning the ULCA was more confessional on paper than in practice. But even on paper it was not very confessional. From the time of its 1920 "Washington Declaration" the ULCA was the leader of ecumenicity in American Lutheranism. Its presidents Frederick Knubel and Franklin Clark Fry were the leading spirits of American Lutheran ecumenism. The inerrancy of Scripture was already thoroughly, but cleverly, compromised by the time of the ULCA's 1938 "Baltimore Declaration."

1) The General Synod

The General Synod was the descendant of the Pennsylvania Ministerium and other eastern synods. Its goal was practical Lutheran unity, based on organizational unity rather than on agreement in doctrine. Already in its early days it blurred distinctive Lutheran doctrines.

2) The General Council

In 1867 The General Council developed as a conservative backlash against the liberalism of the General Synod. The General Council's failure to remain a strong voice for confessional Lutheranism is one of the unhappy stories of American Lutheranism. Despite the strong theological leadership of Charles Porterfield Krauth (d. 1883), the General Council failed to reach complete doctrinal agreement with the more confessional midwestern synods, and it was ultimately resubmerged in the lax theology of the General Synod/ULCA. The General Council's failure to practice biblical principles of church fellowship and doctrinal discipline led to the loss of the generally sound theology of Krauth and others like him.

3) The United Synod, South

The General Synod, South broke away from the General Synod because of the Civil War, not because of confessional reasons. The Tennessee Synod, which joined the General Synod, South in 1886 to form the United Synod, South, had a strong confessional tradition. Although the United Synod, South was somewhat more conservative than the General Synod, it was reabsorbed into the liberal stream of eastern Lutheranism by the ULCA merger of 1918.

b. The Augustana Synod

The Augustana Ev. Lutheran Church was in some respects a latecomer to the liberal Lutheranism of the LCA. The Augustana Synod was the end product of the concern of Swedish mission societies for the Swedes who had come to America in the late 1800s. It had a reputation of being more concerned about doctrine, piety, and missions than the ULCA. However, new faculty members began to introduce historical criticism at its seminary at Rock Island, Illinois, already in the early 1930s. Augustana was submerged into the LCA in 1962.

c. The Danes

The Danes brought an interesting doctrinal heritage into the LCA and ELCA. The "happy" Danes had followed the view that the Apostles' Creed was the true expression of the Word of God, which was only "contained" in Scripture. The happy Danes entered the LCA in 1962. The "sad" or "holy" Danes were noted for earnestness and moral vigor. As the United Danish Ev. Lutheran Church (later UELC) they entered the American Lutheran Church in 1960.

d. The Others

The Slovaks, Icelanders, and Finns did not bring special theological emphases to the united churches.

2. The ALC

The American Lutheran Church contributed two and a half million members and 5,000 congregations to ELCA. The ALC was strongly concentrated in the Midwest.

In some respects the story of the American Lutheran Church is sadder than the story of the LCA because many of the ALC's constituent synods were once much closer to the sound confessionalism of the Synodical Conference than the synods of the ULCA had ever been. Even when the ALC had begun to deteriorate badly, it tried to hold the middle ground between the Missouri Synod and the LCA. The doctrinal compromises necessary to create the Lutheran mergers of the 20th century generally met with much greater resistance in the synods of the ALC family than in the LCA group. Nevertheless, compromise and laxity always prevailed in the end.

When the ELCA merger was first proposed, neither the ALC nor its leadership was very enthusiastic. Differences between the ALC and the LCA which posed some problems to the creation of ELCA were the stronger congregationalism and aversion to bureaucracy in the ALC and the greater percentage of ALC members who were concerned about the inerrancy of Scripture. The ALC also had a much stronger tradition of pietism and lay leadership than the LCA.

The ALC formed in 1960 was the nearly equal merger of the German synods of the old ALC and the Norwegians of the Evangelical Lutheran Church (ELC), with a handful of Danes thrown in for good measure.

a. The Germans—The Old ALC

The predominately German Ohio, Iowa, and Buffalo synods united in 1930 to form the old ALC. The sad fact about the history of this group is how far it deteriorated from the confessional theology which once made this group relatively close to the doctrinal position of the Synodical Conference.

b. The Norwegians

The Norwegians in America have passed through a confusing array of breaks and mergers. However, by 1917 most of them were united into the Norwegian Lutheran Church which was ultimately called the Evangelical Lutheran Church (ELC). The Lutheran Brethren, the Evangelical Lutheran Synod (ELS), the Association of Free Lutheran Congregations, the American Association of Lutheran Churches, and many of the other ALC congregations which refused to enter ELCA are all examples of predominately Norwegian groups which rejected the mergers that ultimately led to ELCA.

1) The Norwegian Synod

The old Norwegian Synod was a member of the Synodical Conference until it withdrew as a result of the election controversy in the 1880s. This withdrawal was not due to rejection of the Synodical Conference's doctrinal position, but was a tactical move to deal with internal differences in the Norwegian Synod. It entered the 1917 merger of Norwegian synods on the basis of a "settlement" of the dispute about election which was no settlement at all, but an agreement to let the two views on election co-exist. The other parties in the 1917 merger were the United Church, which included the Norwegians who had opposed the correct scriptural doctrine advocated by the Missouri Synod during the election dispute, and Hauge's Synod, which had a strong emphasis on personal piety and lay leadership. Our sister synod, the ELS, developed from the part of the Norwegian Synod that refused to enter the 1917 merger. That the Norwegian Synod failed to maintain its stance of confessional Lutheranism is one of the sad stories of American Lutheranism.

2) The United Church

At the time of the 1917 merger which formed the ELC, the United Church was the largest of the three large Norwegian bodies. It occupied the middle ground doctrinally and practically. It aimed to avoid what it regarded as the presumptuous piety of the Haugeans and the authoritarian theology of the Norwegian Synod. By name and design it was intended to be inclusive rather than exclusive.

3) The Lutheran Free Church

The Lutheran Free Church (LFC) split from the United Church in 1897 because of a dispute about the role of Augsburg College and Seminary. The LFC strongly emphasized the autonomy of the congregation and the role of lay leadership. The LFC twice refused to join the ALC of 1960 during the time that its convention had voting open to all adherents of the synod. When a switch was made to a representative form of government, the LFC became a tardy entrant into the ALC.

The ALC in ELCA

It appears that the biggest losers in the ELCA merger were the conservatives in the ALC. Many voices in the ALC were raised against the ELCA merger. The merger was voted down by more than 800 ALC congregations during the ratification process. Yet only about 40 ALC congregations refused to enter the merger and withdrew. Why this great discrepancy?

It appears that the conservative movement in the ALC (and the lesser movement in the LCA) failed to have any significant effect on the merger because it was a house divided from the very beginning. It was a shaky coalition of orthodox Lutherans, fundamentalists, evangelicals, charismatics, neo-orthodox, and people alarmed by the promotion of sexual immorality in the LCA and ALC. There was no true unity on the doctrine of Scripture or on the principles of fellowship. Many of those who held the strongest views on Scripture eventually departed for the American Association of Lutheran Churches (AALC) and a few left for the LCMS, but even they had very inadequate concepts of the biblical principles of fellowship and of the dangers of the charismatic movement. Long before the merger was finalized, many of the conservatives had made it clear that they would go along with the merger even if their views were ignored. This certainly undermined any credibility their testimony might have had. Many charismatics stayed with the merger in the naive hope that their spirituality could somehow revitalize the new church. A significant reason for the failure of the conservative movement to have much impact on the merger may have been that so many of its adherents were more oriented toward personal experience than toward sound doctrinal statements. In the end most of them placed personal ties and group loyalties ahead of doctrine. Many other ALC members sympathized with the moral and doctrinal concerns of the protesters, but they remained silent on the sidelines while the battle was lost. Although a few of those who remain in ELCA contend for biblical truth, a public witness for the doctrine of Scriptural inerrancy has almost been silenced in ELCA.

3. The AELC

In 1976 the Association of Ev. Lutheran Churches was formed as a result of the Seminex dispute in the

LCMS, which was described in the first section of this book. The AELC brought about 100,000 members into ELCA. Its acceptance of historical criticism, of ecumenical ventures, and of ordained women makes it right at home in ELCA.

The AELC had an influence on the merger which was disproportionate to its small size. The AELC was in some respects the catalyst which created the merger, since from the beginning it regarded itself as an interim denomination and issued a call for union already in 1978. The AELC's congregationalism and its demands for a definition of the ministry broad enough to include Christian day school teachers were a significant factor in creating ELCA's conflicts concerning synod power and the doctrine of the ministry, which are discussed below.

Conclusion

When the three synod conventions gave initial approval for the ELCA merger, the AELC approved 136-0, the LCA 669-11, and the ALC 897-87. When discussions and votes were held to implement the merger, there was practically no discussion of doctrine except for a few skirmishes over the inerrancy of Scripture which were quickly squelched. The only other major doctrinal concern during the merger process was the definition of the public ministry. Points of contention were the roles of bishops and deacons and whether the ministry also includes such called workers as Christian day school teachers. When it became clear that this dispute could not be solved by the deadline for the merger, the topic was tabled for five years of further study. The main sources of contention during the final stages of the merger process were funding the pension plan and the location of the headquarters. How could two-thirds of American Lutherans rush to merge with so little concern for doctrine?

Our overview of history makes it clear that the ELCA merger was not much different from most of the previous mergers of American Lutheranism. In one merger after another the more confessional group made its protests, but ultimately went along with the merger, and soon found itself and its theology submerged in the widening liberal mainstream. In almost every case it was *failure to practice the scriptural principles of church fellowship* which led to the absorption and finally the death of confessional theology. In many cases there was godly piety among the conservatives, but it was piety in search of a theology. Without a sound doctrinal foundation and lacking the convictions to break ties with the adherents of false teaching, the protesters had no strength and staying power to resist the juggernaut to merger and doctrinal compromise.

The ELCA merger simply followed the pattern of numerous mergers which had gone before. The only difference was that the nearly universal acceptance of negative historical criticism among the leaders of the ELCA merger made the results more deadly than before. Now the question was no longer, "Will firm confessional Lutheranism survive?" The question now is, "Will basic biblical Christianity survive in the majority of American Lutheranism?" As we will see in the next part of this study, there is good reason to fear that the answer will be "No."

The ELCA merger was driven by special interest groups promoting sexual and political liberation. The quota system for selecting delegates (a selection process that determined commission and board memberships based on gender and race) allowed such groups to dominate the planning commission and the first governing boards of ELCA to a degree disproportionate to their strength within the membership of ELCA. The theologians provided little guidance. They had turned away from such unresolved inter-Lutheran questions as lodge membership, millennialism, the Antichrist, and election and adopted a ceaselessly changing agenda of theological fads. They were more ready to speak of options than to offer scriptural answers to urgent doctrinal and moral questions.

The result is that a commitment to confessional, biblical theology has disappeared from the official levels of ELCA. Some voices still speak out against the more shocking sexual and political theories coming out of ELCA officialdom and against the most flagrantly unchristian and un-Lutheran doctrinal aberrations, but such voices as the Lutheran Forum can be called confessional only in a limited sense. Overall, there is no voice left for biblical Lutheranism at the official level or the seminary level. The only battle left is for the hearts, minds, and souls of individuals at the congregational level.

When we look at ELCA, it is shocking how great the gulf is that separates us from them; but when we look back over American Lutheran history, it is equally surprising how close many of the pieces that make up the ELCA puzzle once were to us. The decline and fall of groups like the General Council, the Ohio Synod, and the Norwegian Synod stand as a strong warning for us to take heed lest we fall.

In the next sections of our study we will see how this decline of American Lutheranism has led to the denial of even the most fundamental doctrines of Christianity. We must fear whether most of American Lutheranism will remain Christian, yet alone Lutheran.

B. The Official Confession of ELCA

At the present time ELCA's official doctrinal position is limited largely to the doctrinal preface of its constitution. There are a number of reasons for this very limited doctrinal position.

One reason, of course, is that in its relatively brief history ELCA has not had time or occasion to declare itself on many doctrinal issues. Official statements will undoubtedly multiply as time goes by.

Another reason for the very limited doctrinal platform is that many in ELCA do not want to have their doctrinal stance too narrowly defined. Very little doctrinal discussion preceded the formation of ELCA. The merging bodies proceeded toward merger with the assumption that they already had a sufficient degree of doctrinal unity to form one church body. This does not mean that they assumed they were in complete doctrinal unity. Quite the contrary, they realized, for example, that they could not reach agreement on the doctrine of the ministry. This lack of agreement could not be allowed to hold up the merger, so it was set aside to be resolved later. In their opinion this disagreement was not fundamental enough to prevent the merger, even though this lack of agreement meant that some called workers had to enter the merger without any assurance of what their ultimate status in the new church body would be.

The only prerequisites for merger were a common confession of faith in the triune God and in Christ as Lord and a constitutional claim of allegiance to the authority of Scripture and to the Lutheran Confessions. Such a paper confession is what the planning commission produced and what ELCA ratified in its *Confession of Faith* (COF).

1. The Trinity

This church confesses the Triune God, Father, Son and Holy Spirit. COF 2

We and many members of ELCA are very happy to see this statement as the foundation of ELCA's confession. This part of the confession we could endorse wholeheartedly, if we did not know what lay behind it. It is clear from the circumstances which surrounded its adoption and from public explanations of it that this confession is whitewash which hides an ugly reality.

First of all, ELCA's confession of the basic principles of the ecumenical creeds and the Lutheran Confessions is intended to give the unwary the impression that ELCA is a church which remains faithful to the doctrinal traditions of the Lutheran church. It is claimed that such a confession makes ELCA a conservative church. Agreement on this basic core allegedly gives the church freedom to differ on other matters (see *The Lutheran,* September 7, 1988, p. 9).

This allowance for doctrinal diversity is bad enough in itself, but there is serious reason to doubt whether even these very basic doctrinal affirmations can be taken seriously. When the planning commission was drawing up ELCA's confession of faith, Elwyn Ewald (AELC) proposed that the words "Father, Son and Holy Spirit" be dropped from the confession to avoid sexually exclusive language. Other representatives opposed the deletion on the grounds that the language is taken directly from Scripture and that deletion of the words could prove offensive at a time when the church's language is in transition. After the opposing viewpoints had been presented, the motion to delete the reference to the persons of the Trinity failed by only three votes, 30-33 (ALC Press Release, February 27, 1984). Debate about the necessity and desirability of using the name of the Father, Son, and Holy Spirit in baptism has continued in ELCA. Some continue to advocate baptism in a gender-neutral name for God. One suspects that ELCA Lutherans have not heard the last of the question of "Father, Son, and Spirit."

2. Christ the Lord

This church confesses Jesus Christ as Lord and Savior and the Gospel as the power of God for the salvation of all who believe. COF 2.02

This article can be understood correctly, and it is soothing to the conservatives in the pew, but its language is vague enough to allow a mixed bag of teachings about Christ and salvation as we shall see later in this study.

3. The Scriptures

The critical doctrinal battle during the formation of ELCA was the dispute about whether the church should retain the doctrine of biblical inerrancy. We must, therefore, examine this issue at greater length. The ELCA confession says:

a. Jesus Christ is the Word of God incarnate, through whom everything was made and through whose life, death, and resurrection, God fashions a new creation.

b. The proclamation of God's message to us as both Law and Gospel is the Word of God, revealing judgment and mercy through word and deed, beginning with the Word in creation, continuing in the history of Israel, and centering in all its fullness in the person and work of Jesus Christ.

c. The canonical Scriptures of the Old and New Testaments are the written Word of God. Inspired by God's Spirit speaking through their authors, they record and announce God's revelation centering in Jesus Christ. Through them God's Spirit speaks to us to create and sustain Christian faith and fellowship for service in the world. COF 2.02

ELCA seminary professor Timothy Lull comments:

> Why is this section so long? Perhaps misunderstanding is likely at this point. In our society "Word of God" is likely to be heard as Bible or Holy Scripture. That is part of the meaning. But Lutherans intend something more than praising the Bible when they attribute faith to the power of the Word. (*The Lutheran,* November 2, 1988, p. 17)

It is clear from sections a and b of the confession and from Lull's remarks that these two sections (although true in and of themselves) are intended to detract from the unique importance of Scripture as the only source of the Word of God which we have available to us today. The confession does not clearly state whether Scripture actually reveals specific, true statements from God or simply conveys testimony about the religious experience of its writers. Sections b and c imply that present-day preaching from Scripture and our act of listening to preaching from Scripture are on the same level as the inspiration of Scripture. These sections minimize the importance of the historical content of Scripture and exalt our experiencing of revelation. That this is deliberate is clear from Lull's commentary on this article:

> Lutherans turn to Scriptures for personal study or community teaching knowing already that at their heart is to be found not many things, but one thing: the saving knowledge of the Triune God revealed in Jesus' preaching. We confess what we have learned there—that God's chief purpose has been to shower love and salvation on us, not primarily to fill us with information nor to make us moral people. These things are in the Bible too, and it is a key task of faith to see how they are related to the central message of Jesus Christ.
>
> For the Bible to be the Word of God in this strong effective sense, it cannot be a dead book—however perfect or inspired. It must be a living medium through which the Spirit moves us to believe the good news that we read there. This is why the Spirit is mentioned both as inspiring the authors—and equally important—as speaking to us "to create and sustain Christian faith."

Some of what Lull says can be understood correctly, but the intention is clearly to reduce the content of Scripture which must be believed to a gospel core and to permit the view that the effect the Bible has on us is more important than what the Bible says. How are believers to relate the moral commands of Scripture to the central message of Scripture about salvation? Are we to use the commands as a guide for gospel-motivated Christian living or may we dismiss them as secondary, unessential matters? How is the historical information in Scripture to be related to the central truth of the gospel? Is it a fictional framework for the message or an account of the real events through which God carried out his plan? Both possibilities are left wide open in ELCA.

The vague, non-committal nature of this confession is clearly illustrated by the two key statements on Scripture:

> *The canonical Scriptures of the Old and New Testaments are the written Word of God. Inspired by God's Spirit speaking through their authors, they record and announce God's revelation centering in Jesus Christ.* COF 2.02

> *This church accepts the canonical Scriptures of the Old and New Testaments as the inspired Word of God and the authoritative source and norm of its proclamation, faith and life.* COF 2.03

The confession twice declares ELCA's loyalty to Scripture as the inspired Word of God. This may deceive the unsuspecting, but anyone who paid any attention to the merger negotiations could see that this wording was a deliberate watering down of the statement concerning Scripture in the ALC constitution, which had included the term "inerrant." There were immediate pleas to retain the concept of inerrancy, but they were decisively rejected. Lull comments:

> What is the ELCA's specific view of the authority of Scripture? The confession simply affirms that the Bible is "the inspired Word of God." Some Lutherans are disappointed that there is no claim that the Bible is infallible, inerrant, or non-contradictory. But it serves us

> well not to rush by "inspired" without considering its strong claim. The ELCA affirms that God has spoken and still speaks through the Bible to bring us to faith. Adjectives are not piled up to emphasize the meaning of "inspired." Instead, the confession makes a sweeping claim about the Bible's function. (*The Lutheran,* November 23, 1988, p. 17)

ELCA's confession is clearly intended to reject verbal, plenary inspiration and to allow for the view that there are many errors in Scripture. As a result of the premerger debate about this section of the confession *The Lutheran* ran an article to explain the intention of this paragraph to its readers (*The Lutheran,* October 15, 1986). After identifying "inerrancy" as a Fundamentalist term borrowed by some Lutherans, the article summarizes the views of the ALC and LCA concerning Scripture.

> When the LCA and the new ALC appeared on the scene in the early 1960s, many people wondered, "Why two churches instead of one?" One reason was a division of opinion over Scripture. The leaders of the churches that formed the ALC insisted on the position their predecessors had taken in 1919 and 1930, when they described the Bible as "the divinely inspired, revealed, and inerrant Word of God" in the constitution of the new ALC. The LCA constitution, on the other hand, shows the influence of the historical-critical approach.

It is clear which approach won out in the ELCA statement. The more liberal ULCA/LCA approach is the clear victor. However, the victory did not require much of a battle, because it is clear that the 1960 ALC confession was a sham from the start. From the beginning the ALC's confession of scriptural inerrancy was merely a ploy to calm the conservatives. Even while the leading theologians were accepting the word "inerrant" in the constitution, they were publicly rejecting its real meaning.

In their efforts to calm ALC conservatives and justify the omission of "inerrancy" from the ELCA constitution, ALC officials explained that the word "inerrancy" in the ALC constitution never had any real and final meaning. In *The Lutheran Standard* (December 12, 1986, p. 14) Lowell Erdahl cited the autobiography of Fredrik Schiotz to substantiate this claim and concluded, "Let's stop scrapping over the ambiguous, confusing, misleading, unnecessary word 'inerrant.'"

The only positive thing that can be said about this whole development is that the former deception and cover-up of historical-critical conclusions about the Bible have been replaced by an open rejection of inerrancy and by an attempt to educate the laity to the "virtues" of critical methods of Bible study. A concerted effort has been made to inform the laity and to win them over to the negative critical method. One can only hope that the ELCA theologians have overplayed their hand and that their open propaganda for their critical views will open the eyes of some lay people and that they will reject the package they have been sold. However, it seems overly optimistic to expect that many ELCA members will be moved to action. Any who had their eyes open should have known what they were getting in the ELCA confession. Its implications were clearly revealed before ratification, yet very few refused to go along with it.

If members of the LCA and ALC were formerly unaware of how completely their theologians have abandoned the inerrancy of Scripture, they no longer have any excuse for such ignorance in ELCA.

The abandonment of any meaningful understanding of inerrancy and the adoption of the conclusions of negative criticism of the Bible are not hidden away in obscure writings of the ELCA dogmaticians. They are being proclaimed in *The Lutheran,* which is intended also for lay people, and in the educational publications of ELCA.

Those who remain in ELCA in spite of this false teaching can hardly claim ignorance as a plausible defense. How heartbreaking that so few are willing to take a stand for the truth!

4. The Lutheran Confessions

Genuine Lutherans teach and defend the teachings of Scripture as they are set forth in the Lutheran Confessions. Does ELCA really deserve the name Lutheran? It claims:

> *This church accepts the Apostles', Nicene, and Athanasian Creeds as true declarations of the faith of this church.* COF 2.04
>
> *This church accepts the Unaltered Augsburg Confession as a true witness to the Gospel, acknowledging as one with it in faith and doctrine all the churches that likewise accept (its) teachings.* COF 2.05
>
> *This church accepts the other confessional writings in the Book of Concord, namely the Apology of the Augsburg Confession, the Smalcald Articles and the Treatise, the Small Catechism, the Large Catechism, and the Formula of Concord as further valid interpretations of the faith of the Church.* COF 2.06

Anyone who knows how flagrantly this fine-sounding confession is disregarded by ELCA theologians will not be impressed by this paper pledge. But even the wording of ELCA's confession contains adequate clues as to its emptiness.

The ecumenical creeds are accepted as "true declarations of faith," but not as the only true teachings, which are binding on all members in a literal sense. The Augsburg Confession is elevated above the other Lutheran confessions as the only confession necessary to establish church fellowship. It is endorsed as "a true witness to the Gospel." Such an affirmation does not require acceptance of all its teachings, only of its gospel message. It also permits other "true witnesses" to be accepted as alternative interpretations of the faith. In a similar way the other Lutheran confessions are accepted as "valid interpretations of the faith," but not as doctrinal statements which are binding on all teachers of the church in all their points.

The series of articles in *The Lutheran* which explained to the laity the significance of ELCA's confession made it clear that acceptance of the Confessions' doctrine was limited. Concerning the Apostles' Creed Lull observes:

> At times Christians may experience discomfort when saying these words. Some people may be puzzled or discouraged by the creed. Perhaps they do not understand the words. Perhaps they understand but they are not sure that they believe. . . . But we can give the impression that our community has no identity and our faith has no content if we are not concerned about what we believe, or if we say only those parts of the creed about which we personally are certain. Reciting the creed puts a helpful pressure on us to be clear about what we believe. This pressure helps us grow into the fullness of the church's faith. (December 19, 1988, p. 17)

Lull claims that the Formula of Concord, Lutheranism's most thorough confession, tends not to settle doctrinal controversies, but to set boundaries for debate (May 3, 1989, p. 15). It is incredible that a dogmatician could make such a statement about the most precise confession ever written. Once the determination has been made to leave the doors open to doctrinal laxity, it seems that no confession, no matter how precise, will be allowed to stand in the way.

Conclusion

It is clear that although ELCA's confession may seem to commit the church to traditional doctrine, in fact, its ambiguous language leaves the door wide open to all sorts of doctrinal diversity, as we shall see in the next section.

C. The Dogmatics of the ELCA

In the previous section we saw the room for doctrinal diversity which the ELCA's confession of faith allows to its theologians. In this section we will examine how this freedom is used by the dogmaticians (professors who teach courses on doctrine) at ELCA seminaries. We will not talk about their views of the Antichrist, lodges, election, objective justification, and other disputed questions from the history of American Lutheranism, since they have long ago given up concern about such issues. We will confine ourselves to examining their teachings on four basic doctrines of Christianity: the nature and sources of theology, the doctrine of God, the person of Christ, and justification. If these doctrines are corrupted, there is little reason to be optimistic about the rest.

Our primary source will be the textbook, *Christian Dogmatics,* which was written by six leading theologians of ELCA in the hope that it would become the standard text for teaching doctrine in their seminaries. This two-volume text, published in 1984, is generally called *Braaten and Jenson* after its two editors, who at that time were professors of systematic, or doctrinal, theology at the Chicago and Gettysburg seminaries. If the approach to doctrine which is typical of this text dominates the seminaries of ELCA, the prospects for the survival of truly Lutheran, biblically-based doctrine in ELCA are bleak indeed.

This text makes for unpleasant reading, not only because of its doctrinal content, but because of the obscure jargon and philosophical language which its authors favor. Nevertheless, it is necessary for us to examine it in order to form an impression of the kind of doctrinal instruction ELCA pastors will receive.

1. The Nature and Source of Theology

Already in the preface the authors state quite frankly that an acceptance of diversity of doctrine in the church is one of their basic presuppositions. They say:

> Although all of us stand within the Lutheran tradition, the differences among us and the consequent inconsistencies in the book are considerable. . . . At some points the authors simply disagree, and this disagreement occasionally reaches the point of contradiction. We leave it to the readers to discover the places where it occurs. (I, xvii)

The sad fact is that for the authors of this book the goal of doctrine is no longer the orderly presentation of the truths revealed in Scripture. Instead the task of the dogmatician is to criticize the doctrinal traditions of the various churches and to make proposals for rewording the teachings of the faith in ways which will be acceptable to advocates of negative criticism of the Bible and to evolutionists. Dogmatics is done not so much to defend the doctrine of the church, but to criticize it (I,5,7).

2. Scripture

It is not surprising that careful study of Bible passages is almost totally absent from Braaten and Jenson's work. Their presentation consists almost entirely of analysis and criticism of the traditional teachings of the churches, followed by their proposal for changing the doctrine to make it more appropriate for today. This approach is the natural result of the authors' rejection of the Scripture as a reliable, authoritative source for dogmatics. Although they call Scripture "the source and norm for the knowledge of God's revelation which concerns the Christian faith," they limit the authority of the Bible for Christian theology to the gospel of Jesus Christ to which the Christian Scriptures bear witness. This is made very clear in the chapter on Scripture, which was written by Braaten.

The introductory thesis for his chapter on Scripture is reproduced here in its entirety:

> The Holy Scriptures are the source and norm of the knowledge of God's revelation which concerns the Christian faith. The ultimate authority of Christian theology is not the biblical canon as such, but the gospel of Jesus Christ to which the Scriptures bear witness—the "canon within the canon." Jesus Christ himself is the Lord of the Scriptures, the source and scope of its authority. (I,61)

Notice that for Braaten the Scriptures are no longer written revelation from God, but the source of knowledge of revelation about faith. This means that Scripture does not reveal facts about God which are the basis for our faith, but tells us about the faith experiences of the apostles so that we can have the same experience. This makes Scripture less than the "very words of God" (Romans 3:2).

We certainly agree with Braaten that the gospel is the heart of Scripture, but all other doctrines serve the gospel. The correct biblical teaching of a specific doctrine must be based on all of the passages which speak about that specific topic, not on some vague personal opinion deduced from a "principle of the gospel." For example, the terrible reality of hell cannot be denied on the basis of the gospel proclamation of God's love, since many other passages clearly speak of hell. The role of women in the church must not be based on imaginative interpretation of some alleged "gospel principle of equality," but it must be based on the passages that specifically address the issue of women's role in the church. Every passage of Scripture is authoritative for the specific topic which it addresses.

A basic premise of Braaten is that the historical-critical method has made the traditional view of the inspiration and inerrancy of Scripture obsolete. His grounds for abandoning the doctrine of biblical inerrancy are the alleged exposure of many errors and contradictions in the biblical text and an alleged desire to avoid elevating the Bible as an idol above Christ. The doctrine of the Word which characterizes *Christian Dogmatics* is that the Bible is the Word of God only in a derived way. The Bible is the Word of God, not so much because it was given by inspiration of God, but because it conveys the message of salvation. According to this view it is not possible to assume the literal historicity of events recorded in the Bible.

Braaten says:

> In modern Protestant fundamentalism [Braaten's term for groups like the WELS], which ironically claims to bear the legacy of the Reformation, the authority of Scripture is extended to include infallible information on all kinds of subjects. Fundamentalist biblicism is rejected by most theologians and is out of favor in most of the seminaries that train clergy for the parish ministry. They reject biblicism not merely because historical science has disclosed errors and contradictions in the biblical writings, but rather because the authority of the Bible is elevated at the expense of the authority of Christ and his gospel. Non-fundamentalist Protestants [i.e. ELCA] also accept the Bible as the Word of God in some sense, but they point out that the concept of the Word of God, as Barth made clear, cannot be confined to the Bible. (I,74,75)

> Today it is impossible to assume the historicity of the things recorded. What the biblical authors report is not accepted as a literal transcript of the factual course of events. Therefore, critical scholars inquire behind the text and attempt to reconstruct the real history that took place. (I,76)

This section gives a pretty good idea of what impression, if any, ELCA seminary students would get of WELS.

Wisconsin Lutheran Seminary certainly cannot be classified among the "great theological schools" by Braaten's standards. ELCA theologians "accept the Bible as the Word of God in some sense." Do ELCA lay people realize this is the real meaning of their confession's statement, "This church accepts the canonical Scriptures as the inspired Word of God"?

Braaten and Jenson reduce the Bible to a source book for the imaginative reconstruction of church doctrine. The disastrous effects of this approach upon any attempt to produce a biblical dogmatics are exposed by a statement which concludes the introduction:

> Critical attention to what the texts actually say has exploded the notion that one orthodox dogmatics can be mined out of Scripture. There are different theological tendencies and teachings in the various texts. Ecumenically this has led to the practical conclusion that the traditional demand for a complete consensus of doctrine may be wrong-headed, if even the Scriptures fail to contain such a consensus. (I,77)

3. The Lutheran Confessions

If this is the treatment accorded to Scripture, we can hardly expect the Lutheran Confessions to receive much better. Braaten states:

> The right wing appeals to the confessional principle to exclude all new developments in modern theology. . . . Here doctrines become laws, creating a climate of doctrinal legalism in the church, snuffing out the freedom which is the church's birthright from the gospel. (I,51)

> Dogmatics can look for insights in the creeds and confessions of the church without being archaistic, and it can learn new ways of thinking without becoming modernistic.

> [The confessions] are not so much a legal requirement as an evangelical witness, not legally binding canonical

norms, but human testimonies of faith in the Word of God. (I,51,52)

Here we see exposed the real meaning of ELCA's confession, "We accept the creeds as true declarations of the faith of this church." According to ELCA the Lutheran Confessions do not bind today's theologians to teach according to them. They merely show us how past generations confessed their faith. They remind theologians not to get too far from the traditional language of their denomination. Lutheran liberals have to sound like Lutherans, Catholic liberals have to sound like Catholics, even if they believe (and disbelieve) the same thing.

Braaten's presentation is certainly a gross distortion both of the true confessionalist's attitude toward the confessions and of the original aims and purposes of the confessions. Neither the confessors of the Reformation era nor their heirs think of the confessions as a law to be enforced on the unwilling. But neither do they think of them as tentative suggestions for the church. The confessions were written to be subscribed to and adhered to by all real Lutherans. They also distinguished Lutherans from other Christians and served as a basis for resolving theological disputes.

Luther and the other confessors would not have been ready to surrender or to declare optional a single article of the confessions unless it would have been proved to them from Scripture that their position was wrong. This is a far cry from the kind of confession offered by Braaten and Jenson who are ready to surrender not only the distinctly Lutheran articles of the confessions, but even the ecumenical trinitarian articles which are their foundation.

4. Trinity

The chapter on the Trinity was written by Jenson. In the spectrum of ELCA it is relatively conservative since it rejects the feminist elimination of "Father and Son" and maintains, "In functional continuity with biblical witness, 'Father, Son, and Spirit' is the proper name of the church's God" (I,87). However, after reading Jenson's presentation one cannot be sure if Jenson believes in the three persons of the Trinity in the traditional sense of the term. I think not. This section, like much of the text, is written in an obscure jargon. Readers cannot help wishing that Braaten and Jenson had remembered that one of the chief goals of theological writing is to communicate clearly. Does Jenson's view clearly communicate the doctrine of the Trinity? Judge for yourself.

> The trinitarian name did not fall from heaven. It was made up by believers for the God with whom we have found ourselves involved. "Father" was Jesus' peculiar address to the particular transcendence over against whom he lived. Just as by this address he qualified himself as "Son" and in the memory of the primal church his acclamation as Son was the beginning of faith. "Spirit" was the term provided by the whole biblical theology for what comes of such a meeting between God and a special human being of his. It is involvement in this structure of Jesus' own event—prayer to the "Father" with the "Son" in the power of and for "the Spirit"—that is faith's knowledge of God. Thus, "Father, Son, and Spirit" summarize faith's apprehension of God. . . . But in the event so summarizable "Father, Son, and Spirit" came together also simply as a name for the one therein apprehended, and apparently did so before all analysis of its suitability. (I,93)

Jenson appears to be claiming that the names "Father, Son, and Spirit" are simply words for describing different ways that we may experience a religious "encounter" with a vaguely revealed divine being. His further elaboration of his theory supports this interpretation.

> "Father, Son, and Spirit" is a slogan for the temporal structure of the church's apprehension of God and for the proper logic of its proclamation and liturgy. (I,99)

For Jenson the names "Father, Son and Spirit" respectively seem to correspond to past, present, and future aspects of religious experience. There are three persons of the Trinity because our religious experience can be thought of as past, present, or future (I,129).

Jenson explicitly rejects the eternal pre-existence of the Second Person of the Trinity:

> Instead of interpreting Christ's deity as a separate entity that always was—and proceeding analogously with the Spirit—we should interpret it as a final outcome, and just so as eternal, just so as the bracket around all beginnings and endings. Jesus' historical life was a sending by the Father, the filial relationship between this man and the transcendence to whom he turned temporally occurred. . . . Truly the Trinity is simply the Father and the man Jesus and their Spirit as the Spirit of the believing community. (I,155)

In later sections of his book Jenson tries to soften or blur the preceding statements. He denies that his teaching implies that the Father and Spirit are created by Jesus and that it destroys all individual terms of the persons. Jenson's method is to make provocative statements like the ones quoted above and then to surround them with a confusing fog of orthodox terms and philosophical jargon. He would undoubtedly be amused by our approach of taking isolated quotations from this presentation and protest that such excerpting is unfair to his overall message and does not catch the subtlety of his thought. But despite his disclaimers to the contrary, Jenson's doctrine of God must be classified as a strange brew of temporal modalism (the belief that God is not three distinct persons, but has different ways of appearing) and process theology (the belief that God evolves along with the world). He effectively denies the clear distinction of the three persons of the Trinity. The most favorable construction one could put on Jenson's work is that he leaves the existence of a personal God in doubt. What a tragedy that the simple proclamation of the triune God found in Scripture and the clear, if somewhat overly philosophical, statements of the early centuries are submerged in obscure theorizing which is neither clear nor simple.

At the mid-point of our dreary journey through *Christian Dogmatics* we find that it leaves us with no dependable source of doctrine and with nothing but vaguely defined religious experience as our god. Braaten and Jenson provide no real knowledge of our creator and no real awareness of the seriousness of sin.

Since the doctrine of theology and the doctrine of God provide foundations for all the rest of theology, errors in these doctrines inevitably affect the whole system of doctrine. If these foundations are shaky, we may expect the whole building to fall. It is, therefore, not surprising that in ELCA there are significant problems with almost every doctrine of Scripture.

But what about the doctrine of the person and work of Christ? Has this doctrine upon which the church stands or fails been preserved in the theology of ELCA? Sad to say, we will see that even this indispensable core of Christianity has been obscured and corrupted by the leading theologians of ELCA. Again we will use *Christian Dogmatics* as our main source.

5. The Person of Christ

The section of *Christian Dogmatics* dealing with the person of Christ was written by Carl Braaten. Braaten begins by describing the method for establishing our belief about Christ:

> Christology is the church's reflection on the basic assertion that Jesus is the Christ of God. Its aim is to construct a comprehensive interpretation of the identity and meaning of the person of Jesus as the Christ, under the condition of contemporary knowledge and experience. (I,473)

> It will always be necessary for the church to test its christological interpretations by referring to the biblical picture of Jesus the Christ. The biblical picture of Christ, however, is not like a single snapshot. It is more like a montage of portraits sketched by several artists, from various angles and at different times and places. For this reason, scholars now speak of a multiplicity of christologies in the New Testament. Nevertheless, all of them stem from the earliest witness of the apostles to Jesus of Nazareth, his life and teachings, and particularly his suffering, death, and resurrection. (I,475)

Braaten sees three basic sources of Christology which do not necessarily agree with each other: what Jesus thought about himself, what the early church preached about Christ, and what the church throughout the centuries has taught about Christ. We must use critical methods to separate Jesus' own views of himself from those of the early church since these two strands are woven together in Scripture.

Since Braaten believes that there is no unified doctrine of Christ in Scripture, it is not surprising that he has trouble producing one of his own. Nevertheless, he goes about the task by analyzing the three sources and then "constructing" his own christology based on those three sources, adjusted to conform to contemporary knowledge and experience. It is not surprising that the Christ that emerges from this process is a pale reflection of the God-man revealed in Scripture and confessed in the creeds of the church.

Consider Braaten's presentation of the true humanity and true divinity of Jesus Christ. We realize all is not well already in Braaten's lead-in to this part of his presentation. He seems to speak of the divine and human natures in Christ as our theological inventions when he states:

> In predicating divine and human natures, as well as divine and human attributes, of the one Lord Jesus Christ, we are giving expression to the knowledge of faith that God has entered history as the power of final salvation of humanity and the cosmos. (I,514)

If we have our doubts whether the statement that "God has entered history as the power of final salvation of humanity and the cosmos" is really the equivalent of the biblical truth that the eternal Word who always dwelt in the presence of the Father became flesh and dwelt among us, all uncertainty is removed by Braaten's explanation of the deity of Christ.

> The confession that Jesus in his person is truly God means that God's decisive and final word to the world has been communicated once for all in his Word made flesh.
>
> The notion of the preexistent Son of God becoming a human being in the womb of a virgin and then returning to his heavenly home is bound up with the mythological picture of the world that clashes with our modern scientific world view. (I,527)

Braaten seeks a middle ground between the conservative's rejection of biblical criticism and the liberal's demythologizing of the Christian faith, which rejects the myth of the incarnation as non-essential to that faith. Braaten accepts the story of the incarnation as a helpful myth which contains symbolical elements which are not to be taken literally, but which has some historical aspects and therefore should be retained in the church (I,528).

The Christ who is invented by Braaten is God in name only, not in essence. Although Braaten tries to retain ties with the traditional Christology (or at least its terms), he so thoroughly redefines them and mixes them with philosophical abstractions that the God-man of Scripture is hidden in a cloud. Although he is willing to call Jesus Christ "God," this cannot be understood in the biblical or creedal sense. Braaten's confession that Jesus is God does not involve the entry of the eternal, preexistent Son into the world by becoming man. For Braaten's "incarnation" means that God somehow presents the message of salvation in Jesus.

> In confessing the true divinity of Jesus Christ, we are saying that in Jesus God is revealed as the finally valid answer to all our ultimate questions about the meaning of existence and the future life. As the exclusive medium of God's final word of judgment and hope, Jesus is the one through whom the knowledge of ultimate salvation enters history. . . . Jesus can be our God because the power of God's absolute future was shown to be effectually present in his person and ministry." (I,538)

> The preexistence of Christ is an integral part of the myth of the incarnation. References to the preexistence of Christ . . . say that Jesus is the eternal Son of God because the salvation he delivered to humankind has its origin in God. (I,545)

With the doctrine of the incarnation so emptied of meaning, it is not surprising that Braaten empties the creedal statements concerning Christ's humiliation and exaltation of their historical content.

a. The Virgin Birth

> The primary interest of dogmatics is to interpret the virgin birth as a symbol and not as a freakish intervention in the course of nature. . . . It is important then

> not to get bogged down in biology, but to read it as a symbol witnessing the truth of the kerygma. The truth of the conception by the Holy Spirit is that God was the author of salvation through Christ from the beginning, not first in his resurrection, nor on the cross, nor at the baptism, but from the moment of his conception by Mary. (I,546)

b. Jesus' Death

> The crucifixion of Jesus happened once and will never happen again. Nevertheless, the meaning of the historical cross was transmitted in the suprahistorical language of mythological symbolism. . . . When the cross is viewed mythologically, and not simply as one historical event alongside others, it receives redemptive significance of cosmic proportions. (I, 547,548)

c. Jesus' Resurrection

> We can call the resurrection an historical event because it happened in a particular place, in Palestine, and at a definite time, a few days after his death and prior to Pentecost. . . . On the other hand, the nature of the reality that appeared to the witnesses was more than historical. It was an eschatological event. (I,551)

What Braaten has left us is an incarnation and virgin birth which are just mythical symbols, a crucifixion which is a means of salvation only when it is mythically interpreted, and a resurrection which has historical reality only in the minds of the witnesses. With foundations like these it is no wonder that many in ELCA believe in salvation detached from the historical deeds of Christ, salvation which can be obtained without knowledge or faith in Christ. If biblical Christianity still exists in ELCA, it is found in the preaching of some faithful pastors and in the hearts of God's captive people. It is not found in the teachings of its chief dogmaticians. But perhaps this verdict is premature. We still have not looked at

Christian Dogmatics' treatment of justification. Since liberal theologians have maintained that the only doctrine necessary for the unity of the church is the doctrine of the gospel, perhaps we will find something better there.

6. The Work of Christ

The doctrine of justification by grace through faith is the central doctrine of biblical and Lutheran theology. It is shocking that *Christian Dogmatics* has no chapter on justification. One would think that to label a book without a chapter on justification as a Lutheran dogmatics or even as a Christian dogmatics would be a contradiction in terms.

Perhaps this should not surprise us since the central place of justification in Christian theology was denied already in Braaten and Jenson's introduction:

> At some points in the history of Lutheranism, a full reception of the catholic dogmatic tradition has been hindered by an attempt of Lutheran confessionalism to deduce the whole of the church's life and teaching from the special principle of Lutheran theology—the article of justification by faith alone. Whenever this reductionist error has been committed, it has produced a particularly inhumane form of Lutheran sectarianism. (I,xviii)

After this statement nothing which follows in *Christian Dogmatics* should surprise us. We should not be shocked that theologians who share the viewpoint of Braaten and Jenson have surrendered the biblical teaching of justification in their dialogues with Rome. "Agreement in the gospel" no longer means acceptance of the biblical, Pauline, Lutheran doctrine that our sins are freely forgiven by the gracious verdict of God, not because of anything which we have done, but solely on the basis of Christ's perfect payment for sin. Today "agreement in the gospel" has been reduced to the belief that somehow or other our salvation is ultimately dependent on God.

Things get no better in *Christian Dogmatics'* main discussion of justification which is contained in Gerhard Forde's chapter entitled "Christian Life." A survey of the highlights (or lowlights) is enough to impress us with how devastating the decline of Lutheran theology has been in ELCA.

Forde cannot come to grips with the biblical concept of justification because he has downgraded the biblical concept of law. For him law and gospel are not distinct biblical teachings which assert certain truths. Law and gospel are defined as two different types of religious experience. Law is defined as "one way in which communication functions when we are alienated, estranged, and bound" (II,400). The doctrine of Christ's payment for sin is stripped of its legal aspects. In his earlier chapter on the atonement Forde states:

> Jesus came and died because God is merciful, not to make God merciful. We killed him because he forgave sins, not to make forgiveness possible.
>
> The historical account is a code, a surface manifestation of a real meaning to be found on a different and transcendent level. The historical event must be translated into eternal truth about the satisfaction of God's honor, or elevated to a sublime example of dedication to whatever religious people are supposed to be dedicated to, or transcribed into a story about the deception of cosmic tyrants. None of that is evident from the event itself. It comes from the moral, mythological and metaphysical baggage we carry with us. (II,79)

With a starting point like this it is not surprising that Forde cannot deal with the legal aspects of the atonement and justification in a biblical manner.

Forde explains the significance of Jesus' death by a parable which is intended to develop a nonreligious concept of sacrifice (II,89). In the parable each of us is represented by the driver of a truck which accidentally runs down Jesus and "splatters him on the front of our machine." What is the meaning of this accident? Listen to Forde's own explanation:

> The one splattered against the front of our truck comes back, to say "Shalom." There is no strange transaction that takes place somewhere in celestial bookkeeping halls to make it universal. The one we killed, the one no one wanted, is raised from the dead. That is all. (II,92)

If that vague parable is all there is to the gospel, what peace is there for troubled consciences? We can only say, God preserve us from "gospel" preaching like this, preaching based on no real payment for sins, preaching with no proclamation of a verdict of forgiveness for all, preaching with nothing to offer except a vague emotional appeal, expressed in unclear jargon and mysterious parables.

In ELCA dogmatics the biblical message that Christ paid for the sins of the whole world and that God has credited that payment to the whole world has been watered down to an ill-defined religious encounter. This is the greatest tragedy of ELCA dogmatics. To those who cherish the clear proclamation of the scriptural doctrine of justification by grace alone through faith alone as their greatest joy and privilege, the thought that two-thirds of the Lutheran pastors in the United States will receive their understanding of justification from a text like this is heartbreaking. Imagine, if you can, having such a pastor instruct your children or grandchildren. Imagine him speaking to the heathen in your behalf. Imagine her comforting you after the death of your husband or wife or visiting you on your deathbed.

The gap between the theologians of ELCA and the theologians of WELS is not just a matter of such doctrines as election, millennialism, lodges, fellowship, and the role of women. It involves the most basic foundations of faith—the doctrine of God and the doctrines of the person and work of Christ. The differences between the theologians of ELCA and the theologians of WELS is greater than the differences between Lutherans and Catholics at the time of the Reformation. We can hardly justify calling the theology of the top theologians of ELCA Lutheran or even Christian.

We can only hope that some pastors and lay people in ELCA will preserve the precious doctrine of justification and the other doctrines of Scripture in spite of the views of their leaders. In our last section, we will see that the leaders of ELCA are making it increasingly difficult for the people to do so.

D. Popular Doctrine

We have seen how the official doctrinal position of ELCA leaves the door wide open for theologians to develop and promote all sorts of doctrinal diversity and how leading theologians of ELCA have used this freedom to overthrow even the most basic doctrines of Christianity. In ELCA concern for doctrine often takes a backseat to church and world politics. On the organizational level of ELCA there is virtually no testimony remaining for confessional Lutheranism.

But are the people in the pew aware of this? Is this doctrinal change being hidden from them as it often is in the earlier stages of the capture of a church by false teachers?

This may have been true in the past. Fifteen years ago, when I served a congregation composed primarily of former LCA members, I was told that the main problem they experienced with LCA preaching was not that it boldly and openly promoted false teaching, but that it did not clearly present the true teaching of Scripture, not even the doctrine of justification. They generally received bland preaching about how good God is and what good people we should be.

Although this analysis still holds true to some degree, in recent years there has been a definite effort to bring the laity up-to-date with recent doctrinal developments in ELCA. Even before the merger both the LCA and ALC had programs to introduce and popularize the historical-critical approach to Scripture among the laity. In 1984 the ALC produced a series of essays published under the collective title *The Doctrine of the Word in the Lutheran Church.*

This document was sent to all congregations as part of the premerger effort to win acceptance of the historical-critical method. The ALC's Search and the LCA's Word and Witness programs were other efforts toward this goal. Prior to the merger *The Lutheran* and *The Lutheran Standard* published numerous articles to increase the acceptance of the historical-critical method among the laity.

To assess how this campaign is proceeding in ELCA we will consider four sources: the doctrinal leadership provided by the presiding bishop, popular moral teaching, preaching, and the publications for the laity.

1. Bishop Chilstrom

For better or for worse, the doctrinal direction of a church will be influenced by its leader. As the first bishop of the ELCA, Herbert Chilstrom has had a unique opportunity to influence the direction of the new church. Unfortunately, his position on Scripture was made clear in an interview published even before the merger was complete.

> The prescriptive method [of using Scripture] is based on the assumption that Scripture is used to discover final answers to questions. Thus, when confronted with a particularly thorny issue, one could go to Scripture,

> study carefully every text that addresses the issue and come up with a conclusive response. Scripture as "norm" means Scripture as answer book.
>
> I suspect that most of us in the LCA come at these matters from the descriptive method. We see Scripture as no less important. . . . But for us "norm," means "guide" rather than "rule." Having informed ourselves of what Scripture has to say, we go on to ask questions about other ways in which God may be trying to enlighten us. (*The Lutheran,* March 21, 1984)

In the interview Chilstrom expressed the opinion that his view of Scripture is "very conservative." With theological leadership like this, is it any wonder that the troops are confused and doctrinal chaos reigns?

2. Popular Moral Teaching

We have not yet given any consideration to another major factor in the decline of ELCA. Special-interest lobbies whose primary interest is not doctrine, but the promotion of certain political, social, racial, or sexual goals, have a very powerful influence in the machinery of ELCA.

A recent example of this is provided by the 1991 and 1993 draft statements on sexuality which were circulated by the Division for the Church in Society of the ELCA. These study documents are allegedly a preliminary step toward developing a sexual ethic "faithful to Scripture and tradition, which is nevertheless responsive to issues of our day."

These drafts have caused an uproar, because they appear to condone homosexuality and extramarital sex. Although posing as study documents, the ELCA studies are really an appeal to the members of ELCA to take a fresh and sympathetic look at homosexuality and extramarital sex and to refrain from judging such actions if they are practiced in a loving, committed way.

The following evaluations of the 1991 document are cited from the February 3, 1992, issue of *Lutheran Forum,* a newsletter which promotes "confessional Lutheranism" in ELCA. They thus give an "insider's view" of the document.

ELCA pastor Tom Brock comments:

> The people of my congregation are angry and I am personally embarrassed to be a Lutheran. I expected more of my church than the lies we get from sexologists on the Phil Donahue Show.

ELCA Pastor Leonard Klein comments:

> The publication of this recommendation of sin is as such a sin. This is no invitation to dialogue. It is a farewell to the Scripture principle. It is an act of war against the Christian faith.

Those are pretty strong statements. Are they justified by the content of the ELCA document?

Klein continues:

> You know you are in trouble early on when the preface says in the second sentence that this study is designed to stimulate "dialogue with Scripture." Some of us thought that in such issues we were to be led, formed and instructed by Holy Scripture. . . . At the outset, then, the problem is clear. The long held belief of most Christians that there is in fact already a quite identifiable Christian teaching about sex is swept away in the eagerness to "hear the voices." And in the interest of hearing the voices, Scripture is turned into a weak partner in the cacophony at the table and displaced as the sole rule and norm. . . . Repeatedly through the document, standard positions on sexual ethics are listed alongside other options with no hint that one has or should have any priority. Our document . . . manipulates. It presents false and misleading options in the most pleasant of language.

Concerning homosexuality the 1993 document says:

> No passage specifically addresses the question facing the church today: the morality of a just, loving, committed relationship between persons of the same sex.

Among the members of ELCA three responses are common:

> Response 1: To love our neighbor who is homosexual means to love the sinner, but hate the sin.
>
> Response 2: To love our neighbor means to be compassionate toward gay and lesbian persons and understanding toward the dilemma facing those who do not have the gift of celibacy.
>
> Response 3: To love our neighbor means open affirmation of gay and lesbian persons and their mutually loving, just, committed relationships of fidelity.
>
> Response 1 needs to be questioned on biblical and theological grounds, indeed challenged because of its harmful effect on gay and lesbian people and their families. Responses 2 and 3 are strongly supported by responsible biblical interpretation. (*The Lutheran,* November 1993, p. 32)

Conspicuous by its absence from these paragraphs is any mention of repentance and forgiveness. These could be read into Response 1, but this is the response which the document challenges.

These ELCA study documents are a frontal attack on biblical, Christian morality. Some might call them a sneak attack, but their intentions are not very well disguised. They aim to overthrow the authority of Scripture as the only norm for establishing doctrine and morals.

We share the anguish which many members of the ELCA suffer from these documents, as well as their embarrassment to have the name Lutheran associated with documents like these. But ELCA members should not be surprised by the documents. Before the ELCA merger was finalized, its leaders' views on Scripture were clear. Lip service to the authority of Scripture could not whitewash the ugly reality revealed by ELCA's explicit rejection of biblical inerrancy. There was no secret about the political and sexual agendas of the special interest lobbies hiding behind the quota system which ELCA used for choosing their representatives on boards and committees. Some blame the ELCA's present sad situation on the quota system. There is an element of truth to this claim, but the heart of the problem lies elsewhere. *The universal dominance of the negative critical approach to Scripture in ELCA* has destroyed lay people's confidence in the clarity and authority of Scripture. When critical methods of Scripture study reduce the moral statements of Scripture to a collection of contradictory, culturally-biased opinions from unknown authors, is it any surprise that the church can reach no moral conclusions? The present confusion about moral issues in ELCA is a natural outcome of its leaders' acceptance of negative critical approaches to Scripture. These study documents on sexuality are a natural fruit of critical approaches to Scripture.

3. Periodicals

An important source for informing the laity is the official church magazine. The answers which people receive to their doctrinal questions in that periodical are an important barometer for them of their church's doctrinal position. What impression are people getting from *The Lutheran?* I have selected a few questions and answers from the "Since You Asked" column of *The Lutheran,* written by Norma and Burton Everist. The questions and answers which follow are condensed from the original.

> Question: Is it true Jesus was born so he could die on the cross?

Answer: Jesus was born not to die, but to live for us. If Jesus was born simply to die, Herod's soldiers could have killed him as a baby. The cross is central to our preaching because it shows the depth of God's love for us. . . . Some preaching describes Jesus' death as a payment to God's wrath. This approach stresses guilt as a barrier to our entry into heaven. There is truth here, but this is only one of many ways the Scriptures proclaim the meaning of Jesus for us. (March 30, 1988, p. 46)

Question: Is it now considered naive or even heresy for Lutherans to believe that Adam and Eve were real people?

Answer: For centuries the church believed in the actual existence of Adam and Eve. Recent scholarship suggests that the significance of the Adam and Eve stories is not their literal truth or lack of it but the theological points they make about the creation of humankind in God's image.

If someone believes Adam and Eve were historic people, and this view is helpful to their Christian life, it is not good ministry to rip such a viewpoint from them. Nor should the faith of those who understand these stories in a symbolic way be questioned. (June 22, 1988, p. 42)

Question: There are rumors in my congregation that ELCA does not believe in the inerrancy of the Bible. Is this true?

Answer: Please gently correct those who believe the rumors you have heard because they are false. . . . The framers of the [ELCA] confession, following the insights of many Lutheran theologians, believe that this is a more accurate understanding of God's intention for the Scriptures than the term inerrancy. The non-Lutheran, 19th century concept of inerrancy leads to many unhelpful misunderstandings and questions like inerrant in what way? Is the Bible inerrant in matters of history? genealogy? astronomy? These questions lead us directly away from the Scripture's purpose, which is to declare Christ, that we might believe and be saved. The Bible is the source and norm of the church's life, not because it gives us unerring information, but because God continues to speak through it. (July 13, 1988, p. 46)

Question: Some Lutheran churches do not ordain women, using 1 Timothy 2:15 as their primary justification. How can ELCA ordain women in light of this?

Answer: Paul in 1 Timothy reflects the desire to continue the customs in which he had been trained before his conversion. He failed to see the full meaning of his own witness (Galatians 3:28). He was misled by the Pharisaic tradition. . . . We do an injustice to Paul and to this text if we elevate his pastoral counsel to a divine, unchangeable law. But this inspired scripture does teach us how pastors counsel their people. (November 23, 1988, p. 46)

Not all the advice provided by this column is as dangerous as that cited above, but it is clear that ELCA members looking for solid doctrinal guidance cannot expect to find it in *The Lutheran*.

4. Preaching

Certainly in a body as large as the ELCA, there will be a great variety of preaching. One ELCA pastor I interviewed told me to expect ELCA preaching to range from "very conservative to unrecognizable as Lutheran." The following comments are based on my study of 27 sermons preached by ELCA pastors. It hopefully provides a fair example of what can be expected from ELCA preaching.

None of the 27 sermons was based on an exposition of a biblical text. Often no sermon text was read, but the sermon was based on a thought derived in some way from the Gospel of the day. The usual format was that of a lecture or inspirational talk. In general, the sermons were well written and well delivered, and many people would find them interesting and appealing. Obscure jargon like that of Braaten and Jenson was very rare in the sermons I gathered from ELCA churches. Vehement, bold denials of basic doctrines of Scripture were rare. The most flagrant example, a blasphemous denial of hell, was from a published sermon, not from one of the sermons I heard. About one-third of the sermons had explicit doctrinal errors. Among the errors were the denial of hell, implicit denial of a personal devil, denial of male headship, confusion concerning the means of grace, denial of the biblical doctrine of church fellowship, "accepting Jesus as Lord," and praising doubt as a virtue. Doctrinal "sins of omission" were more frequent. None of the 27 sermons contained an explicit, clear presentation of the truth that Christ has made a full payment for our sins, and God has, therefore, declared the world forgiven.

Most of the sermons were moralizing. That is, they called for greater sanctification in some specific area of life, but they provided little or no gospel motivation for the change which they called for. In the ELCA, kindly sermons of the "be good people" type are very common, but so are "prophetic messages" which sharply admonish the hearers to change their ways. There are regular admonitions to deny yourself and frequent warnings against "cheap grace."

The following catalog gives a taste of ELCA preaching.

- A Christmas Eve sermon on Luke 2 entitled "Christmas Memories and the Miracle of Life" talked about the miracles of memory, water, bread, and our lives, but not about the miracle of the incarnation and the virgin birth. "Consider this: the fact that you are here . . . the breath of life you breathe, that in itself is miracle enough. The rest is celebration."

- A Good Friday sermon on John 1 described Jesus' death in detail appropriate to a medical journal and concluded "It was not an easy death," but offered no gospel.
- An Easter season sermon on Thomas's doubt, "Thank God for Doubt," identified those who don't doubt with the likes of Jim Jones, Rev. Moon, gurus, Stalin, Hitler, the Ayatollah, terrorists, and the Posse Comitatus. In ELCA preaching there is often a preoccupation with dealing with doubt.
- Moralizing sermons against a promiscuous lifestyle, against materialism, against prejudice and labeling people, against anger, and against alcohol abuse are common.
- A pro-life sermon based on the sanctity of all life probably was not standard ELCA fare.
- Jesus at Nain was used as a model for compassion and doing good.
- A sermon on Matthew 15:21-28, "Who are the Dogs?", took off on the word "dogs" in the story of the Canaanite woman. It concluded, "It was only recently and in my generation that Roman Catholics and Lutherans could openly worship and share the gospel with one another without judgment and criticism, and still we have a long way to go. In fact our church is unique in its relationship to the local Catholic parish. Your willingness to worship Christ in their house as well as your own, I believe, makes God very happy. . . . Whenever we exclude someone from our family of faith, for whatever reason, we are treating them like dogs, that is in the biblical sense—Jesus makes that point emphatically in today's Gospel."
- A sermon on the suicide of a gifted teenager twice referred to his baptism as a basis for hope, but otherwise spoke little of the grace of God. The focus was on forgiving him, forgiving God and forgiving ourselves, setting aside bitterness, and beginning to live again.

- In ELCA preaching there is frequently a confusion concerning the relationship of the suffering of a Christian and the will of God. ELCA preachers often deny that a Christian's sufferings can in any sense be the will of a good God. In Christ God suffered along with us. We now share in God's suffering. He sympathizes with us and turns evil to good.
- A sermon on Psalm 51 and Luke 15, entitled "God's Repentance": "When God plans to bring evil against sinners, he reminds himself of who he is. When God looks at sinners in Christ, he remembers who he is and doesn't trash us as we deserve. How do we respond? Not so much with sorrow over sin, not so much with a promise to do better, but by rejoicing in his grace. God in Christ has changed his mind. Let's be happy and say, 'Yea, God.' Amen."

This was the best gospel sermon I heard, but does it take sin seriously or present any real payment for sin? Isn't this the very "cheap grace" ELCA claims to fear?

5. Devotional Periodicals

I also read six months of *Christ in Our Home,* Augsburg Publishing House's family devotional booklet. In general the comments made about ELCA preaching apply to these devotions as well. Moralizing predominates.

- The "saints" commemorated in the devotional calendar include Florence Nightingale, Bernard of Clairvaux, Augustine, John Bunyan, Nikolai Grundtvig, Albert Schweitzer, Dag Hammarskjöld, John of the Cross, Teresa of Avila, Francis of Assisi, William Tyndale, Paul Gerhardt, and Henry Muhlenberg.
- "God in love for us made his Son the payment for our disobedience, the restitution for our sin. The sting of death is but a temporary wound." "Jesus came bringing peace with his very life. Jesus became the reconciler, making peace by the blood of the cross." This was the clearest gospel in 27 sermons and 180 devotions. Several other fine statements

occurred in the month's devotions authored by this pastor. However, he could also write that the fullness of God dwelling in Christ (Colossians 1:18-20) is love.

- 1 Timothy 2:1-8: "God's offer is an unconditional pardon for sinners through the Son, Jesus Christ. We respond, "Yes, Lord, I receive you and believe that your salvation, your pardon restores our relationship." The second best gospel.
- On the narrow door: "Those who cannot let go of sin and accept forgiveness will not enter the narrow door. There is an urgency to our being reconciled to God and with all people. The kingdom will be populated with people who have learned to live in peace and love here on earth. Jesus is the one who can bring this about." The third best "gospel," but isn't this a conditional gospel, dependent on our actions?

ELCA preaching is not totally lacking of the gospel, but the gospel is too often smothered by moralizing, false doctrines, and vagueness. The most serious failure of ELCA preaching is not the explicit denial of biblical teachings (although this is all too common), but the almost complete absence of objective justification.

Forgiveness of sins is too often preached as flowing from an arbitrary grace of God without a real objective payment for sin. The truth that Christ's death on the cross was a payment for sin is treated as just one theory about the meaning of his death.

Although certain sins are condemned, the list is usually selective, and there is too often a lack of real gospel motivation for sanctification. There is frequent confusion of law and gospel. I am sure ELCA preachers would be shocked by this judgment, but based on a fairly large sample of ELCA preaching, I must conclude that ELCA preaching is strongly legalistic, that is, it tries to change behavior without adequate gospel motivation drawn from the atoning death of Christ. There is too often a tendency to speak of faith as a decision which we must make.

6. The Lord's Supper

Although the ELCA does not have altar and pulpit fellowship with all churches, for all practical purposes it has totally open communion. Some local ELCA congregations offer open invitations to communion without any limitations or qualifications. Not even a belief in the real presence of Christ's body and blood is required for attending. However, one congregation I visited had the following announcement:

> Holy communion is open to those who accept the real presence of Christ.

This sounds like a limitation until "real presence" is understood in the light of the statement of another ELCA congregation:

> Every baptized person who trusts the promise and presence of Jesus Christ in this meal is welcome at the Lord's table. Our Lord promises that when bread and wine are set aside, blessed, and offered to us to eat and drink and received by us in faith, he is present in us.

Is there any Reformed church in the world that could not accept this statement? It does not refer to the presence of Christ's body and blood with the bread and wine, but only to Christ's presence in the hearts of believers. No wonder intercommunion between ELCA and the Reformed is near!

Conclusion

The picture of ELCA's doctrinal position which we have seen in this study is not a happy one. The leading theologians of the ELCA have not only abandoned confessional Lutheranism. They attack and undermine even the most basic teachings of Christianity. Although there is lip service to Scripture and the Lutheran Confessions, the doctrines which they confess are not maintained in the ELCA. In the regular services and instruction, the teachings of Scripture are often obscured by ambiguity or by false statements.

We can only pray that as long as the Scriptures are heard and the sacraments are administered, the Lord will preserve a remnant in the ELCA and that some will be awakened to come out of her. The sad state of the ELCA calls for confessional Lutherans to redouble their efforts to sound a clear call to authentic Lutheranism at a time when its testimony has almost been silenced in the largest Lutheran church in America.

Comparison of WELS and ELCA*

Scriptural Teachings Maintained by WELS	Samples of the False Teachings Tolerated in ELCA
1. The Bible is the inspired, errorless Word of God.	1. The Bible contains many errors.
2. Jesus' words and actions as reported in the gospels are true history.	2. Jesus did not do or say many of the things reported in the gospels.
3. Genesis 1–3 is a factual, historical account. Adam and Eve were real people.	3. Genesis 1–3 is a myth.

*This list of comparisons is not meant in any way to be complete. As this chapter has brought out, pastors and theologians in the ELCA are permitted to question and deny just about every doctrine of Scripture. This list only highlights some of the major differences between WELS and ELCA.

Scriptural Teachings Maintained by WELS	Samples of the False Teachings Tolerated in ELCA
4. Jesus' death was a true payment for all our sins.	4. The theory that Jesus' death was a payment for sin is one of several theories which could explain his death.
5. Eternal life is possible only through faith in Christ.	5. It is possible to be saved without faith in Christ.
6. Extramarital sex and homosexuality are sins.	6. Extramarital sex and homosexuality may be all right if practiced in a loving relationship.
7. Churches must agree on all doctrines of Scripture before they can practice church fellowship together.	7. It is not necessary or possible for churches to agree on all doctrines of Scripture.
8. It would be contrary to scriptural principles for a woman to serve as a pastor.	8. What the Bible says about the role of women in the church has no authority today. Women may serve as pastors.

For Further Reading

Brug, John F., "The Doctrinal Position of ELCA," 1989. Five essays available from the files of Wisconsin Lutheran Seminary Library. A more detailed version of the information in this book.

Krause, Richard A., "Higher Criticism and ELCA," *Wisconsin Lutheran Quarterly,* Vol. 89, Fall 1992, pp. 243-265.

Leppien, Patsy A. and J. Kincaid Smith, *What's Going On among the Lutherans?* Milwaukee: Northwestern Publishing House, 1992. A very detailed doctrinal study.

Webber, David Jay, "Is the Evangelical Lutheran Church in America Truly Lutheran?" Mankato, MN: ELS Board of Publications, 1988. Brief pamphlet.

PART THREE

WELS AND Other Lutheran Church Bodies in the USA

American Association of Lutheran Churches
Apostolic Lutheran Church of America
Association of Free Lutheran Congregations
Church of the Lutheran Brethren
Church of the Lutheran Confession
Concordia Lutheran Conference
Eielsen Synod
Estonian Evangelical Lutheran Church
Evangelical Lutheran Federation
Evangelical Lutheran Synod
Fellowship of Lutheran Congregations
International Lutheran Fellowship
Latvian Evangelical Lutheran Church
in America
Lutheran Churches of the Reformation
Lutheran Confessional Synod
Protéstant Conference
World Confessional Lutheran Association

PART THREE

WELS and Other Lutheran Church Bodies in the USA

American Association of Lutheran Churches (AALC)

Congregations that resisted the creation of the Evangelical Lutheran Church in America (these were from the American Lutheran Church, for the most part) formed their own fellowship in 1987. At that time there were 68 such congregations. Another 50 refrained from joining the AALC but were sympathetic in one way or another.

Statistics from 1989 show 76 congregations and about 15,000 members. Headquarters are in the Twin Cities and the leader is the Rev. Dr. Duane R. Lindberg.

Standing on the Scripture's inerrancy, this church body hopes to train its future pastors in theologically conservative seminaries but to guide the venture through their own nearby "houses of studies."

This Association has shared roots in the former Lutheran Free Church with the Association of Free Lutheran Congregations which emerged in the 1960s. It chose, however, to develop a fellowship of its own. The reason for this may be found in the AALC's own explanation of its origin as being a convergence of three strands of Lutheranism, namely, orthodox, evangelical, and charismatic. The inclusion of the latter strand sets this grouping apart from most other Lutheran church bodies.

Apostolic Lutheran Church of America

Finnish Lutherans in this country can be cast into several general groupings. The Suomi Synod participated in the LCA merger and its members are now in the Evangelical Lutheran Church in America. Congregations in what was called the Finnish National Church, for the most part, entered the Lutheran Church—Missouri Synod. One of these, in the Upper Peninsula of Michigan at Hancock, is now in fellowship with the WELS.

When Finnish Lutherans, who had been influenced by the Laestadian revival in their homeland, came to this country, they either remained relatively unorganized or grouped themselves into the Apostolic Lutheran Church of America in the late 1920s.

The services of this church body are simple. The Bible is the authoritative guide. A stress on the universal priesthood of believers shows itself in the practice of confession and absolution and in the tradition of lay preaching. The stress on personal piety resulted in the membership requirement of total abstinence from alcoholic beverages.

Most recent statistics of the church body report 57 congregations and 34 pastors. There are more than 7,700 baptized members but only about 3,000 believers who enjoy the privileges of full membership in the local congregation. The church body has published a pamphlet titled *Finnish Apostolic Lutheran Church of America: Constitution and By-Laws.*

Association of Free Lutheran Congregations

This is the largest of the church bodies described in the third part of this publication, with a membership of over 27,000. There are more than 200 congregations and 175 pastors. It has world missions in Central and South America. The church headquarters are in the Twin Cities.

In 1960, when the first American Lutheran Church was merging with the other member churches of the American Lutheran Conference, one conference member refrained from joining the merger until several years later. This was the Lutheran Free Church, a church with Scandinavian (mostly Norwegian) roots.

Shortly before the entrance of the Lutheran Free Church into the American Lutheran Church in 1963, a number of its congregations, concerned about the future of their church body in the ALC, withdrew and formed what they called the "Lutheran Free Church (Not Merged)." This name had to be changed because of a court order and became instead the Association of Free Lutheran Congregations.

Since then other congregations, which withdrew from the larger church groupings in the concern for a more theologically conservative Lutheranism, have joined the association. This process speeded up when the Evangelical Lutheran Church in America was forming in the 1980s.

The association publishes the *Lutheran Ambassador* and has a seminary in the Twin Cities.

Church of the Lutheran Brethren

This church body, with headquarters at Fergus Falls, Minnesota, has some 200 congregations in the Midwest and on both coasts. There are about 13,000 baptized members served by a clergy of about 225 ordained pastors. Communicant members are the confirmed who have had a personal conversion experience and conform their lives to the church's standards.

The church was formed in 1900 at Milwaukee by several United Norwegian congregations dissatisfied with their United Norwegian Lutheran Church and by other like-minded congregations. From the first there was a desire to maintain "biblical congregations" by ongoing church discipline.

There are striking differences between the WELS way of worship and the typical services of the Lutheran Brethren. These services are largely nonliturgical and emphasize lay participation. There are no clergy vestments or altars as we know them.

A strong characteristic of the Church of the Lutheran Brethren during the century of its existence has been its very extensive effort in world missions. The mission fields in Africa, Japan, and Taiwan have more members than does the home church. It is not unusual for the brethren to allocate almost half of the total church budget to world missions.

Those who want to know more about this unique Lutheran church body can find information in its attractive periodical, *Faith and Fellowship*. A full-length diamond jubilee history was published in 1980 at Fergus Falls. Joseph H. Levang wrote the book titled simply *The Church of the Lutheran Brethren.*

Church of the Lutheran Confession (CLC)

Those forming this church body in 1960 were for the most part former members of the Wisconsin Synod. Their reason for withdrawing was that the Wisconsin Synod had allegedly been "marking" the Missouri Synod as an erring church body but continued to be in fellowship with the errorists in the Synodical Conference. Using the language of Romans 16:17 from the King James Version, the withdrawers insisted that once a church body was "marked" as causing divisions and offenses, the "avoiding" should begin without delay. The Wisconsin Synod, on the other hand, maintained that when false doctrine was detected in a sister church, there could still be a need and opportunity for the scripturally enjoined admonition of the erring. Fellowship should be terminated as soon as it becomes clear that the sister church is persisting in its error.

That was the basic cause for the division in 1960 and remains so now, long after the Wisconsin Synod terminated fellowship with Missouri in 1961 and withdrew from the Synodical Conference in 1963. In the early 1990s discussions between representatives of the CLC, the ELS, and the WELS demonstrated that this disagreement was still a barrier to any reunion or mutual recognition of fellowship. Although representatives of the three church bodies were able to agree on a joint statement on the role of admonition in the termination of church fellowship, the CLC continued to insist that there was a doctrinal difference between the WELS and the CLC. WELS representatives maintained that there was agreement on the principles of church fellowship, but a difference of opinion about whether the WELS had properly applied those principles in the 1950s and 60s. An account of these discussions can be found in the 1993 WELS *Reports and Memorials,* pp. 232-241.

The Church of the Lutheran Confession has a membership of less than 9,000 in its 70 churches. There are some 80 ordained pastors. The worker-training school is located in Eau Claire, Wisconsin. Publications are the *Lutheran Spokesman* and the theological quarterly, *Journal of Theology.*

Concordia Lutheran Conference

In the middle third of this century when the Lutheran Church—Missouri Synod turned away from the historic fellowship principles and practices of the Synodical Conference, there were protesters in the sister synods of the conference and also in the Missouri Synod itself. In 1951 some of the latter, with a few of the former, formed the Orthodox Lutheran Conference. In 1956 dissension within its ranks led to the withdrawal of some of the members, who a year later organized themselves as the Concordia Lutheran Conference.

This church body took its stand on the Scriptures and the Lutheran Confessions and on the Missouri Synod's *Brief Statement* of 1932 as a basis for Lutheran church union. The strict application of fellowship principles which caused the break with the Orthodox Lutheran Conference continues to keep this little church body isolated from other Lutherans.

According to the latest available statistics, the Concordia Lutheran Conference has five pastors serving some 350 members in five congregations scattered from Illinois to Oregon. The periodical of the church body is the *Concordia Lutheran*.

Eielsen Synod

If the smaller Lutheran church bodies were arranged in order of size from the smallest to the largest or in order of time from oldest to youngest, the Eielsen Synod would have first place in both lists. It was organized in 1846, four years before there was a Wisconsin Synod. Latest but not current reports showed some fifty members in two congregations located in the Minnesota towns of Jackson and French Lick. The last ordained pastor died in 1982, but the remaining members, following the old synodical emphasis on lay preaching, resolved to carry on.

In the tradition of his spiritual father, Hans Hauge of Norway, Elling Eielsen gathered Norwegian immigrants to the Midwest into congregations and the congregations into a synod, the Evangelical Lutheran Church in America, more popularly identified as the Eielsen Synod. The founder, Eielsen, was long in evangelistic zeal but short in organizational ability. There were split-offs from the synod in 1848, 1856, and 1876, the last involving the creation of the well-known Hauge Synod that in 1917 participated in the large Norwegian merger which became known as the Evangelical Lutheran Church.

Much of the strife and division in the Eielsen Synod revolved around the old membership requirement: "No one ought to be accepted as a member of our body, except he has passed through a genuine conversion or is on his way to a conversion." The crowning loss for the body came when its official name was pre-empted by the largest of all Lutheran mergers, ELCA, which began its official existence in 1988.

A closing caution is in place. This church body, if it has not already done so, could at any time pass from the scene.

Estonian Evangelical Lutheran Church

Originally organized in Sweden during the World War II era, the Estonian Evangelical Lutheran Church has a United States district with about 7,000 members, not including a similar number in Canada. There are some 40 congregations in the two countries. No confirmed membership totals are reported.

In contrast to its Latvian counterpart, the Estonian Evangelical Lutheran Church did not join the Lutheran Council in the USA. But like the Latvian Lutherans, these Estonians want to maintain their national Lutheran church at least for the time being. It remains to be seen how the recent independence of Estonia will affect this church.

Evangelical Lutheran Federation (ELF)

Five congregations with some 500 members make up this little, theologically conservative church body that organized in 1977. The congregations are scattered, with one each in Indiana, Michigan, New York, Ohio, and Washington. Since 1977 there has been little change in the size of the group.

In the early 1980s the ELF strongly opposed to masonic lodges, broke its ties with the World Confessional

Lutheran Association, then known as the Conservative Lutheran Association, and with its Faith Lutheran Seminary. The ELF espouses an "exclusionary" lodge practice and insists that a merely "educative" approach is not an adequate policy.

This is the latest available headquarters address: President Ervin C. Dobberstein, P.O. Box 477, Kingston, WA 98346.

Evangelical Lutheran Synod (ELS)

In 1993 the Evangelical Lutheran Synod celebrated the diamond jubilee of its founding in 1918. In that year a small minority in the Norwegian Synod protested the merger of that body into what became the Evangelical Lutheran Church, later a part of the American Lutheran Church and eventually of the Evangelical Lutheran Church in America. The main point of the protest was the merger's compromise in the doctrines of conversion and election.

The church body numbers more than 21,000 members, 150 pastors, and 100 congregations. Its Bethany Lutheran College and Bethany Lutheran Theological Seminary are located in Mankato, Minnesota. Two years after its founding the Evangelical Lutheran Synod (then known as the Norwegian Synod of the American Evangelical Lutheran Church) joined the Synodical Conference and thus cemented a fellowship with the Wisconsin Synod that has lasted through the years and finds expression these days in the ELS—WELS Evangelical Lutheran Confessional Forum.

The Evangelical Lutheran Synod in 1955 terminated its fellowship ties to the Lutheran Church—Missouri Synod and in 1963, along with the Wisconsin Synod, withdrew from the Synodical Conference. It participated with the WELS in the 1993 founding of the international Confessional Evangelical Lutheran Conference.

For more information about this church body consult the diamond jubilee publication, *Built on the Rock,* and Theodore Aaberg's 1968 history, *A City Set on a Hill.* The church paper, *Lutheran Sentinel,* is issued monthly. The theological journal is the *Lutheran Synod Quarterly.*

Fellowship of Lutheran Congregations

The Fellowship of Lutheran Congregations is another church body which formed in protest against theologically liberal developments in the Lutheran Church—Missouri Synod. It was organized in 1979 by midwestern congregations.

Presently the fellowship has five congregations with 500 members. Its paper is *The Voice.* The latest headquarters address is: President Robert J. Lietz, 320 Erie Street, Oak Park, IL 60302.

International Lutheran Fellowship

The "International" in the name does not refer to the geographical spread of the church body at the present time, but rather to its commitment to "go into all the world and preach the good news to all creation." The International Lutheran Fellowship consists of three midwestern congregations with a total membership of 350.

The latest, though not current, statistics give this headquarters address: President E. Edward Tornow, 387 East Brandon Drive, Bismarck, ND 58501.

Latvian Evangelical Church in America

As the name indicates, this is an ethnic Lutheran grouping. Counting the Canadian connection there are some 20,000 members in some 75 congregations.

In the 1950s a loose federation of Latvian Lutherans in this land was formed. Out of it grew the more centralized church body organized in the mid 1970s.

While the Latvian Lutherans were building their organization, there were contacts with the Wisconsin Synod. In Milwaukee, for example, Latvians were granted the use of worship facilities of Wisconsin Synod congregations. Eventually, however, the Latvians found their way into the Lutheran Council in the USA and presently have membership in the Lutheran World Federation and the World Council of Churches.

This may be the place to mention that the European neighbors of the Latvians, the Lithuanians, have several congregations in North America, two in the Chicago area. One of these is a member of the Lutheran Church—Missouri Synod and the other is independent. It will be recalled that the Wisconsin Federation (1892–1917) and the Synodical Conference once sponsored mission endeavors among Lithuanians in our land.

Lutheran Churches of the Reformation

In 1964 several members of the disbanded Orthodox Lutheran Conference (see Concordia Lutheran Conference) and like-minded Missouri Synod dissidents formed the Lutheran Churches of the Reformation. The plural form in the name is important. This church body is determined to uphold the long-standing Missouri Synod position that the one and only God-ordained form of the church is the local congregation and that the pastorate of the local congregation is the one and only God-ordained form of the gospel ministry.

In the early years of this church body's existence there were doctrinal discussions between its representatives and those of the Wisconsin Synod. Although many shared positions in doctrine and practice surfaced, the differences in views regarding church and ministry proved an insurmountable barrier to any kind of church fellowship.

The latest available statistics are incomplete. They report 14 congregations and ten pastors but no membership totals are included. This church body is in full doctrinal agreement with the Illinois Lutheran Conference, a group of six ordained pastors and five congregations located in Illinois, Michigan, Minnesota, and Missouri.

The periodicals of the Lutheran Churches of the Reformation are *One Accord* and the *Faithful Word,* a theological journal.

Lutheran Confessional Synod (LCS)

During 1994 a new church body was formed to serve as a haven for confessional congregations leaving the ELCA. According to the ELCA constitution, it may be difficult for a congregation to leave ELCA and become independent. If the congregation wishes to take any property with it, it must name the church body it intends to join. The LCS gives such confessional congregations, which are not yet ready to join one of the existing Lutheran bodies, a synod to join if they leave ELCA for confessional reasons.

Pastor Randy DeJaynes and his congregation of Decatur, Illinois, led the way in the founding of this group. The group has an announced intention to establish fellowship with the WELS and ELS. Since this group is just getting organized, it is not yet clear how successful it will be in establishing itself as a viable, solidly confessional body.

Protéstant Conference

In the 1920s a protest movement within the Wisconsin Synod resulted in the creation of the Protéstant Conference consisting at that time of some three dozen pastors and teachers and about the same number of congregations. A number of conflicts within the group in 1930, 1952, and 1964 diminished the original ranks considerably. The 1991 statistics reported seven congregations, nine pastors, and 825 members, of whom 250 are confirmed members.

The original protest was provoked by a board-faculty conflict at the ministerial worker-training school, Northwestern College at Watertown, Wisconsin, in which the board set aside a disciplinary action of the faculty and because of which two faculty men resigned their posts. Charges of "rank officialdom" intensified after two Fort Atkinson parochial school teachers were suspended after clashing with their pastor over what they deemed laxity in congregational discipline. When the Western Wisconsin District in 1926 upheld the suspensions, 17 members protested and denounced the action. Soon they and others of like mind were forming a grouping of their own which they chose to name the Protéstant Conference.

Meanwhile in September 1926, Pastor William Beitz read a conference paper, "God's Message to Us in Galatians: The Just Shall Live by Faith," which brought the protests to a head. The paper was a spirited indictment of the status of church life in the Wisconsin Synod. The controversial nature of the paper called forth an official seminary faculty opinion, called *Gutachten,* which found the Beitz paper in error in the matter of mixing justification and sanctification, of demeaning the role of the law in repentance, and of judging hearts. Soon the Beitz paper and the seminary *Gutachten* became the focal point of the worsening conflict.

At Easter time 1928 the newly formed Protéstant Conference began to issue *Faith-Life,* a periodical that is still being published. In the early 1960s a major peace effort was mounted. At the request of the WELS synodical convention the Western Wisconsin District withdrew the original resolutions that suspended Protéstants. Nothing was achieved, however, by way of ending the controversies. In the 1980s, in fact, two Wisconsin Synod pastors joined the Protéstant Conference and a Green Bay congregation split over the issue.

World Confessional Lutheran Association (WCLA)

In 1980 this church body, then named the Conservative Lutheran Association, officially organized after Central Lutheran in Tacoma was expelled by the American Lutheran Church for continuing on its staff a clergyman not certified by the larger church body. The real beginnings, however, date back to 1960 and the formation of the second American Lutheran Church.

Theological conservatives at that time protested trends in the emerging church body, such as a departure from Scripture inerrancy and an espousal of ecumenism. The periodical, *Lutherans Alert—National,* dates back to that time.

In 1987 the World Confessional Lutheran Association, the name adopted in 1984, invited congregations not minded to enter the proposed Evangelical Lutheran Church in America to join the WCLA. Membership figures, however, indicate little, if any, resultant growth. The 1991 statistics list ten congregations with 1,700 members.

Tacoma, Washington, is the location of the Association's Faith Lutheran Seminary; of Central Lutheran Church, a bellwether congregation of the church body; and of its headquarters and president, the Rev. Dr. Reuben H. Redal.

Concluding Notes

The 17 church bodies discussed in this section may be categorized as follows:

Groups originating primarily from protests within the Wisconsin Synod: Church of the Lutheran Confession and the Protéstant Conference.

Groups originating primarily from protest within the Missouri Synod: Concordia Lutheran Conference, Fellowship of Lutheran Congregations, and Lutheran Churches of the Reformation.

Groups originating primarily from protests within the American Lutheran Church and its antecedent bodies: American Association of Lutheran Churches, Association of Free Lutheran Congregations, Church of the Lutheran Brethren, Evangelical Lutheran Federation, Evangelical Lutheran Synod, International Lutheran Fellowship (?), and World Confessional Lutheran Association.

Groups of independent origin: Apostolic Lutheran Church in America, Eielsen Synod, Estonian Evangelical Lutheran Church, Latvian Evangelical Lutheran Church.

Although "American" Lutheranism is used in this study in the narrow sense of Lutheranism in the USA, a note is in place on affiliations of the three largest Lutheran bodies with churches in Canada. The Wisconsin Synod has a handful of Canadian congregations, which remain members of the nearest WELS district in the USA. The Missouri Synod's sister church in Canada, the Lutheran Church—Canada, numbers 80,000 members. ELCA's sister church, the Evangelical Lutheran Church in Canada, has 206,000 members.

Conclusion

In general, we could say that Lutherans in America established churches which were much stronger than the churches they had left behind in their homelands. America was the world center of strong confessional Lutheranism. To a considerable degree this is still true.

Nevertheless, there has been a significant deterioration since the First World War. The negative, critical method of Bible study followed the immigrants over from Germany and wormed its way into their churches in America. As they are now embodied in ELCA, those Lutheran groups whose lax principles of church fellowship and doctrinal latitude on such issues as millennialism and the lodge were enough to mark them as the left wing of American Lutheranism now have moved much farther over to the left fringe of Christianity (and perhaps beyond) as they surrender even the most basic teachings of Christianity. The LCMS, which once formed the bulk of strict confessional Lutheranism, now tolerates a position and practice on fellowship closer to that of the old "American Lutherans" than to that of its forebears. The WELS, which once was just a small appendage on the body of strict, confessional Lutheranism, now finds itself as the largest strictly confessional group.

Early in this century about two-thirds of American Lutherans were adherents of the "moderate" confessional Lutheranism practiced by the predecessor bodies of ELCA. About one-third were members of bodies which practiced the strict confessional Lutheranism of the Synodical Conference. Today about two-thirds of American Lutherans belong to ELCA, which tolerates the most extreme departures from the historic Lutheran faith. Most of the remaining third are members of the LCMS which has slid toward the "moderate" position, formerly occupied by the predecessors of the old ALC. The strict position of the old Synodical Conference, once the most influential voice in American Lutheranism, is now advocated by only about 4 percent of American Lutherans.

Except for the ELS, the small Lutheran bodies are separated from the WELS by differences concerning the old inter-Lutheran issues of church and ministry and church fellowship and by such new issues as charismatic gifts.

The chief causes of this deterioration have been lax fellowship principles and practices and the inroads of the higher critical method of Scripture study. Unless the remaining confessional groups hold firm in resisting deterioration in these areas, it is inevitable that they will slide down the slippery slope of doctrinal decay as so many church bodies have done in the past. We can be warned by the decline of American Lutheranism to "take heed lest we fall."

Appendix 1:
Lutheran Merger Charts

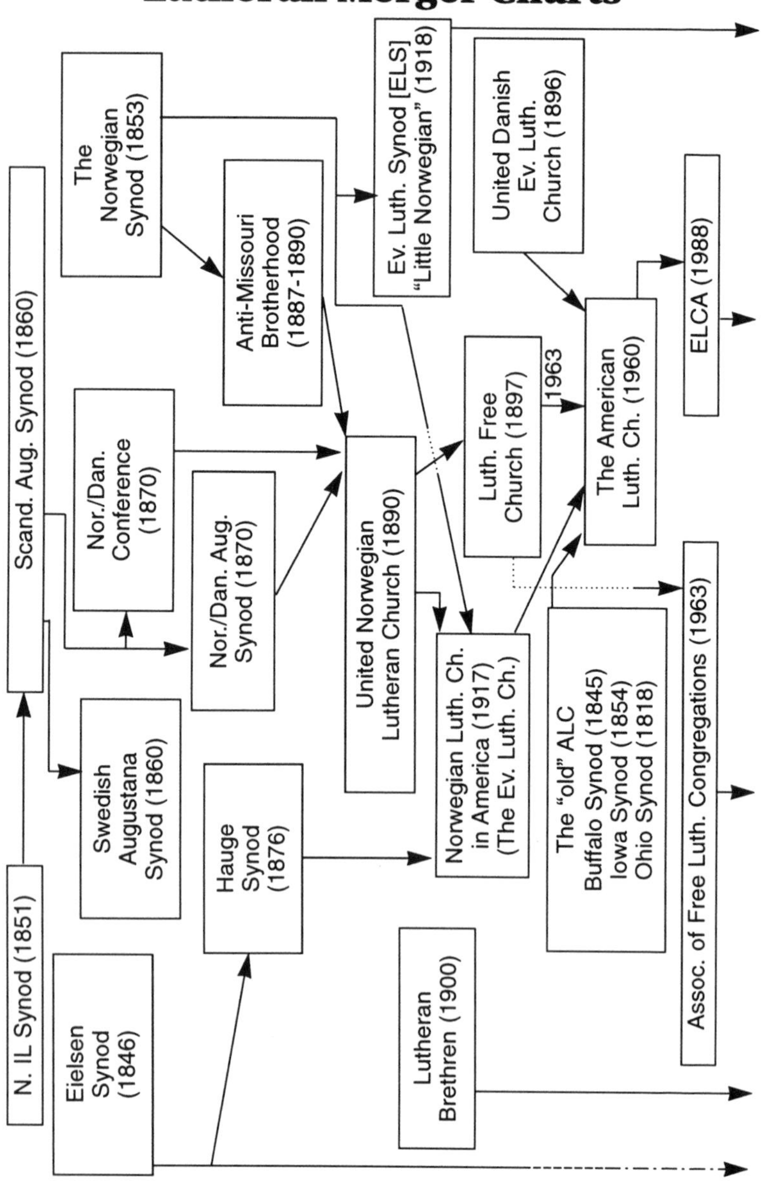

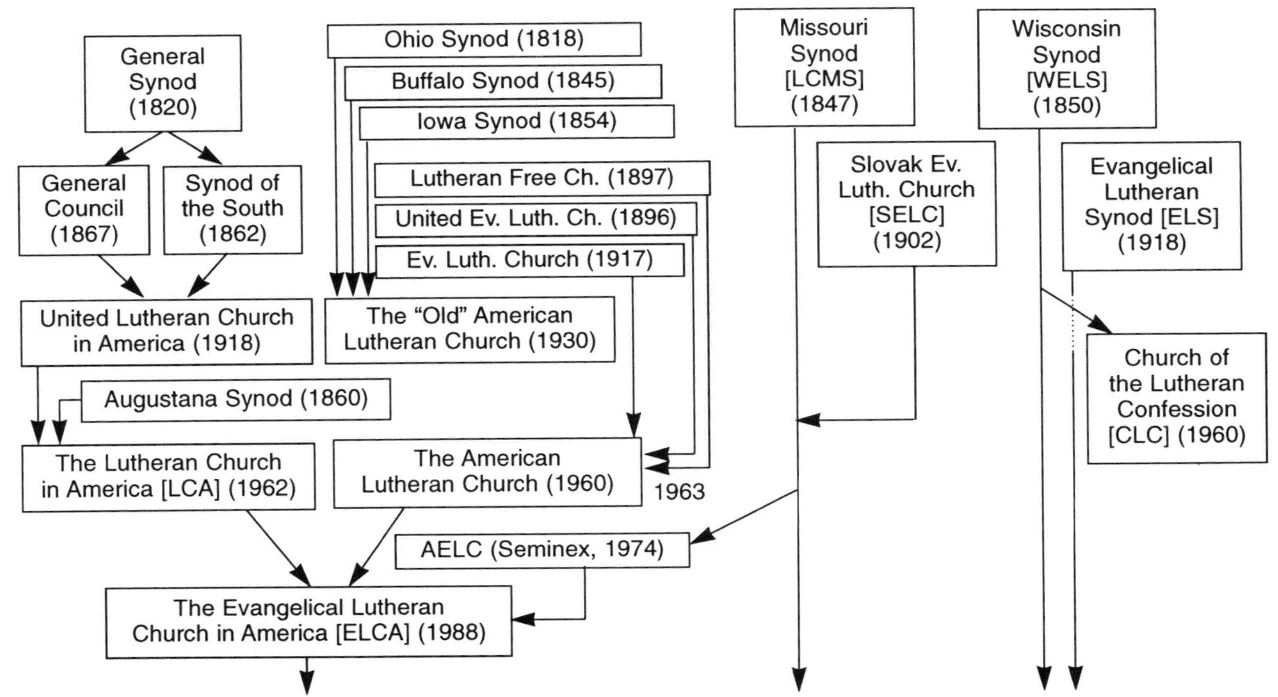
General Synod (1820)
General Council (1867)
Synod of the South (1862)
United Lutheran Church in America (1918)
Augustana Synod (1860)
The Lutheran Church in America [LCA] (1962)
Ohio Synod (1818)
Buffalo Synod (1845)
Iowa Synod (1854)
Lutheran Free Ch. (1897)
United Ev. Luth. Ch. (1896)
Ev. Luth. Church (1917)
The "Old" American Lutheran Church (1930)
The American Lutheran Church (1960)
1963
AELC (Seminex, 1974)
The Evangelical Lutheran Church in America [ELCA] (1988)
Missouri Synod [LCMS] (1847)
Slovak Ev. Luth. Church [SELC] (1902)
Wisconsin Synod [WELS] (1850)
Evangelical Lutheran Synod [ELS] (1918)
Church of the Lutheran Confession [CLC] (1960)

Appendix 2:
Statistics for 1991:
Lutheran Church Bodies in the United States and Canada

CHURCH BODIES	Ordained Ministers	Ministers Serving Congregations	Congregations	Baptized Members	Confirmed Members
1. Evangelical Lutheran Church in America	17,421	9,953	11,074	5,245,177	3,890,947
2. American Association of Lutheran Churches	78*	61*	106	20,171	14,830
3. Apostolic Lutheran Church of America*	34	25	57	7,707	2,995
4. Association of Free Lutheran Congregations	177	122	207	27,571	21,064
5. Church of the Lutheran Brethren of America	224	128	120	12,815	NA
6. Church of the Lutheran Confession	82	57	70	8,722	6,363
7. Concordia Lutheran Conference*	5	5	5	358	208
8. Conservative Lutheran Association	NA	NA	10	1,700	1,410
9. Estonian Evangelical Lutheran Church†	36	29	37	13,278	NA
10. Evangelical Lutheran Federation	4	2	4	507	390
11. Evangelical Lutheran Synod	152	103	126	21,347	16,004
12. Fellowship of Lutheran Congregations	5	3	5	450	370
13. International Lutheran Fellowship*	4	3	3	350	285
14. Latvian Evangelical Lutheran Church†	56	40	73	19,836	17,843
15. Lutheran Churches of the Reformation	10	9	14	NA	NA
16. The Lutheran Church—Missouri Synod	8,389	5,393	6,218	2,615,567	1,958,839
17. The Protéstant Conference	9	6	7	825	250
18. The Wisconsin Evangelical Lutheran Synod	1,643	1,206	1,222	421,189	317,793
TOTAL United States	28,329	17,145	19,358	8,417,570	6,249,591
1. Evangelical Lutheran Church in Canada	859	486	659	206,240	148,641
2. Lutheran Church—Canada	352	251	321	78,566	58,792
TOTAL Canada	1,211	737	980	284,806	207,433
GRAND TOTAL United States and Canada	29,540	17,882	20,338	8,702,376	6,457,024

Statistics as of December 31, 1991
NA = not available
* = indicates prior year data
† = statistics include congregations in Canada

Compiled by Office of the Secretary, Rosters and Statistics
Evangelical Lutheran Church in America